IS “CO… E” A *DIRTY* WORD?

Many would tell you it is. The conservatives are “reactionary,” they want to “turn the clock back,” and this is the worst of crimes in the best of all possible worlds.

But is everything really just fine, and getting better every day in every way? Are all the values and accomplishments of the past ready for the scrap heap?

Professor Mario Pei, who came to this country as a boy when the American dream was a waking reality, has his own answers to these questions. You owe it to yourself—and your country—to read his brilliant, outspoken, deeply moving book.

“The young dissenters cannot have the least idea of the idealistic base of . . . America. . . . Professor Pei will, perhaps, introduce a grain of sand into their memory, which will grate upon their neatly-reciprocating illusions”

—from the Introduction by

William F. Buckley, Jr.

THE AMERICA WE LOST

The Concerns of a Conservative

MARIO PEI

With an Introduction by
William F. Buckley, Jr.

SIGNET BOOKS
A Signet Book
Published by The New American Library

Library of Congress Catalog Card Number: 68-28112

This is a reprint of a hardcover edition published by The New American Library, Inc., in association with The World Publishing Company, 2231 West 110th Street, Cleveland, Ohio.

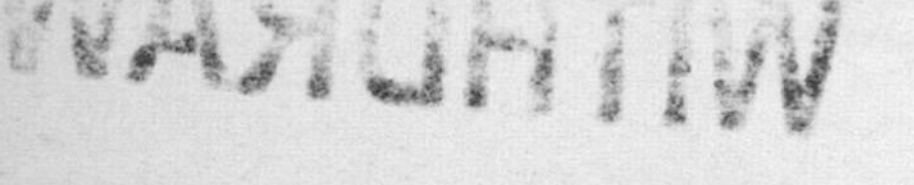

SIGNET TRADEMARK REG. U.S. PAT. OFF. AND FOREIGN COUNTRIES
REGISTERED TRADEMARK—MARCA REGISTRADA
HECHO EN CHICAGO, U.S.A.

SIGNET BOOKS are published by
The New American Library, Inc.,
1301 Avenue of the Americas, New York, New York 10019

First Printing, May, 1969

PRINTED IN THE UNITED STATES OF AMERICA

CONTENTS

III. INTERNATIONAL RELATIONS

IV. TAXATION AND FINANCE

V. EDUCATION

VI. ETHICS, PUBLIC AND PERSONAL

Introduction to the Signet Edition

I APPROACH THE INTRODUCTION TO THE PAPERBACK edition of Professor Pei's lugubrious little book on the transformation of America as among other things an opportunity to welcome, gratefully, that love-of-country which Mr. Pei so keenly, so contagiously feels. He feels that devotion notwithstanding that America is changing in directions undesirable. Immediately one asks, "undesirable" from whose point of view? Well, undesirable, just to begin with, to the man who classifies the changes as undesirable. And undesirable, presumably, to those others who agree with his diagnosis. And, finally, undesirable to still those others whom he can persuade, by the force of his argument, to come along, so that we might lament together the things that have gone by.

It should I think at this point be stressed that Mr. Pei is a very rare observer of America's passage through history. How many others of us arrived here before the First World War and moreover did so, as Mr. Pei's parents apparently did, hounded by the bureaucratic encrustations of the country we fled? And, arriving in America in the same year that Theodore Roosevelt turned over the reins of government to William Howard Taft, experiencing—as how many of us can, even empathically, bring ourselves to experience—what Mr. Pei calls so nostalgically, so simply (he writes like Guy Lombardo) the "freedom-laden air" of America. That description is nowadays so terribly disconcerting. There are, to begin with, the purists who will want to strike it down for linguistic reasons. Surely "laden" implies, at the very least, a "load." But if the spirit thrives on freedom, then are not the mechanical properties of freedom rather uplifting than down-putting? If freedom is buoyant and exhilarating, is it proper to describe it as laden—and by deduction depressing?

But Mr. Pei does not seem to mind at all. He is renowned as a master of language, having written not only dozens of books about a dozen modern languages but, presumably to hone his etymological memory, such books as *The Language of the Eighth-Century Texts in Northern France.* So that when he says "laden with freedom" he means exactly that, and manages to give off the fragrance of freedom as a liberating burden, an oxymoron which the architects of American society would have accepted as altogether routine—because they understood the high cost of freedom. I think of Lincoln at Gettysburg who wondered whether a country devoted to the proposition that all men are born free could long endure; I think of Professor Michael Oakeshott of the London School of Economics who believes that what happened back there a few centuries ago after the breakup of feudalism was that the people decided that the cost of freedom was too heavy and therefore evolved into individuals *manqués,* who now clamor for relief from the responsibilities of freedom and turn to state welfarism, to state authoritarianism; away from parliamentary government, on over to popular government.

And then (the critics of Mr. Pei would continue), just what did he mean in 1912 by "freedom"? Freedom for the Negro? Freedom for the factory wage-earner? Freedom for the helpless conscripts for President Roosevelt's colonialist policies? Freedom for the ghettoized Jew? For the Catholic in the KKK-ridden South? All of that, rather dreamily, escapes the explicit attention of Mr. Pei: not because he is unaware, and not because he is, as the term now puts it, a pig. A pig I understand to mean someone totally plugged in to the Establishment, which Mr. Pei is not, the Establishment being anti-Pei, and Pei being anti-Establishment—so that it might be more accurate to designate him a pig *manqué.* He is in the tradition of those who say what they want to say about society altogether conscious that they are speaking in broad paradigms.

They are quite aware, and absolutely reconciled that the *New York Review of Books* and the academic journals will not bother to weigh their words at all, so never mind hewing to the socially self-conscious little distinctions that appease their reviewers. He is to the conservative movement what, say, Ammon Hennacy was to the pacifists: simple, direct, unembellished, steadfast; and, in that quiet, effective way, deeply refreshing. Exhilarating because his prose, like that of say, Mr. Hennacy, or Dorothy Day, makes no concessions at all to the psychedelic demands of literary fashion. Would you believe, in a public letter of remonstrance addressed to a lady with an infant in tow, carrying an antiwar placard, that he is capable of such a sentence as "Life is not the greatest boon, little lady with the baby carriage"—which essay he concludes by admonishing, "Think it over, pretty little lady with the poster and the chubby baby." Chubby! As I live and breathe!

It would be a mistake to assume that Mr. Pei is altogether conventional in his political and philosophical preferences. His chapter called "Why Not Try Democracy?" will strike some American conservatives as absolutely hair-raising in its recommendations. He is altogether himself (that too is very very rare), and reports on the American situation exactly as he sees it, even when he finds himself allied on this or that point with people whose general positions he finds totally abhorrent. But the lapses are rare. Mostly he hates or distrusts the things that American liberals like and confide in. So they can safely read this book in anticipation of a wholehearted disagreement with it. They will not be disappointed.

Mr. Pei touches on a number of subjects under such general headings as "Education," "Communism," and "Ethics, Public and Personal." A typical entry, under "The Philosophy of Government," is a little essay called Why Not Turn Back? He begins it by a little parable and then goes on to accost head-on the notion that you cannot turn the clock back, a decree which is used more often than any other to oppose what some would believe to be true reform. Mr. Pei goes doggedly to work on it and in a very few paragraphs leaves us with the permanent conviction that the injunction "you cannot turn the clock back" is, among other things, intellectually disreputable.

In a work of great profundity and scholarship, *The Constitution of Liberty,* Professor F. A. Hayek confesses to the same sense of exasperation when up against that jejune commandment. It is as if, he observed, one were told that one could not profit from one's mistakes. If that were the case, life would indeed be brutish and very very short. And Mr. Pei picks up the theme by begging us to reconsider the cliché and strive to maneuver around it. How many examples are available! The passengers trains dwindle, so that now a passenger cannot ride from New York to upper New England or take a sleeper from San Francisco to Los Angeles—not because there are no potential passengers but because the lines cannot charge them at the rate at which they would need to charge them in order to make passenger service profitable. And the reason why they cannot is because there is a derelict bureaucracy in Washington called the Interstate Commerce Commission which presumes to tell the bankrupt railroads how they may bargain with free men. But if one calls for abolishing the ICC one is setting the clock back. Indeed, setting it back to the day when Americans could, if they chose to do so, ride to their destinations on a train. We know about the agricultural subsidies of five, six, seven billion dollars: a most distinguished professor confided to me recently that there is probably not extant one responsible intellectual who could justify the program. But we do not repeal it because to do so would be to set the clock back. So it is with a lot of little regulatory agencies and agencies of general subvention—one thinks of the Rural Electrification Agency. And so many others. Indeed, Mr. Pei makes one deeply conscious that true reform would consist in reaching back to forms we overthrew, either because there was once a need to overthrow them or because we felt experimentally the call to do so: which forms, if now we returned to them, would grant us manifest social blessings and private pleasures. The trouble with the slogan "you cannot turn the clock back" is that it is used metaphorically but the words carry an iron mechanical authority. If the sayer means, literally, You cannot turn back the clock, then the appropriate answer is, Neither can you raise the dead: which is irrelevant to our conversation. If the sayer means by it, You cannot reintroduce legislation which yesterday you repealed, the answer is, Utter nonsense. But much of what Mr. Pei is concerned to do is precisely that—to show what utter nonsense lies in so many of the superstitions codified during his long experience with America.

Moreover, his book raises the question of whether it is any longer possible to talk elatedly about America's historical accomplishments. I mean, to talk about America to a general (which now means critical) audience as one might talk about an elderly lady one loves. I note the title of a recent book by Ralph de Toledano, *America, I Love You.* I do believe, though I have not inquired into the particular circumstances, that the publishers of that volume most probably raised more objections to the title than they would have done if an author had submitted a book called *America, F—— You.* Granted that Mr. Pei's book may prove psychologically acceptable to America's denigrators if only because it does, after all, express disappointment in the way America has evolved. His disappointment with America is the single redeeming quality of the book, as far as these chappies are concerned—notwithstanding their disappointment that he is disappointed about the wrong things.

What Mr. Pei does is to evoke an America which is recognizably different from the America we now have and the America toward which we are so furiously tending. Toward that other, freedom-laden America, he feels a very ardent affection, and he desires us to know why he does. And in the course of telling us, he describes, oh so simply, so absolutely guilelessly, a society which postulated the undeniable individuality of—the individual. Now, it may be that we have learned from modern sociology and modern psychology and modern political science that a society based on individualism never was, and never could, really, be. But I think it important to continue to read the arguments—or, if you prefer, the impressions—of those who thought a) that it was so; b) that it should be so; and c) that it might yet again be so. Because that way we can find out something about the passions that animated a great many Americans in days gone by. Absent that understanding and we are left with historical truncations such as make possible the deracination of the New Left. The young dissenters cannot have the least idea of the idealistic base of the other America. Professor Pei, the sophisticated scholar of languages new and old, attempts here an evocation of that other America, which he poses for us in the style of American Gothic. He may not—almost surely will not—convert the skeptics. But he will, perhaps, introduce a grain of sand into their memory, which will grate upon their neatly reciprocating illusions and perhaps provide the only contact with that emancipating reality which Professor Pei knew so palpably when as a little boy he disembarked in New York City and encountered a nation which by his love of it he continues to honor.

—William F. Buckley, Jr.

I

The Philosophy of Government

The America We Lost

WHEN I FIRST CAME TO AMERICA, IN 1908, I LEARNED A new meaning to the word "liberty"—freedom from government.

I did not learn a new meaning for "democracy." The European country from which I came, Italy, was at that time as "democratic" as America. It was a constitutional monarchy, with a parliament, free and frequent elections, lots of political parties, and plenty of freedom of religion, speech, press and assembly.

But my native country was government-ridden. A vast bureaucracy held it in its countless tentacles. Regardless of the party or coalition of parties that might be in power at the moment, the government was everywhere. Wherever one looked, one saw signs of the ever-present government—in the uniforms of numberless royal, rural and municipal policemen, soldiers, officers, gold-braided functionaries of all sorts. You could not take a step without government intervention.

Many industries and businesses were government-owned and government-run—railroads, telegraphs, and the sale of salt and tobacco among them. No agreement, however trivial, was legal unless written on government-stamped paper. If you stepped out of the city into the country and came back with a ham, a loaf of bread or a

Originally published in *Saturday Evening Post,* this piece was reprinted in dozens of newspapers and periodicals, and anthologized in several books. Reprinted as a clipping of note by the Foundation for Economic Education, it was ordered in the millions of copies by individuals and firms.

bottle of wine, you had to stop at the internal-revenue barriers and pay duty to the government, and so did the farmers who brought in the city's food supply every morning. No business could be started or run without the official sanction of a hundred bureaucrats.

Young men did not dream of going into business for themselves; they dreamed of a modest but safe government job, where they would have tenure, security and a pitiful pension at the end of their plodding careers. There was grinding taxation to support the many government functions and the innumerable public servants. Everybody hated the government—not just the party in power, but the government itself. They had even coined a phrase, "It's raining—thief of a government!" as though even the evils of nature were the government's fault. Yet, I repeat, the country was democratically run, with all the trappings of a many-party system and all the freedoms of which we in America boast today.

America in those days made you open your lungs wide and inhale great gulps of freedom-laden air, for here was one additional freedom—freedom from government.

The government was conspicuous by its very absence. There were no men in uniform, save occasional cops and firemen, no visible bureaucrats, no stifling restrictions, no government monopolies. It was wonderful to get used to the American system: to learn that a contract was valid if written on the side of a house; that you could move not only from the city to the country, but from state to state, and never be asked what your business was or whether you had anything to declare; that you could open and conduct your own business, provided it was a legitimate one, without government interference; that you could go from one end of the year to the other and never have contact with the national government, save for the cheery postman who delivered your mail with a speed and efficiency unknown today; that there were no national taxes, save hidden excises and import duties that you did not even know you paid.

In that horse-and-buggy America, if you made an honest dollar, you could pocket it or spend it without having to figure what portion of it you "owed" the government, or what possible deductions you could allege against that government's claims. You did not have to keep books and records of every bit of income and expenditure or run the risk of being called a liar and a cheat by someone in authority.

Above all, the national ideal was not the obscure security of a government job, but the boundless opportunity that all Americans seemed to consider their birthright. Those same Americans loved their government then. It was there to help, protect and defend them, not to restrict, befuddle and harass them. At the same time, they did not look to the government for a livelihood or for special privileges and handouts. They were independent men in the full sense of the word.

Foreign-born citizens have been watching with alarm the gradual Europeanization of America over the past thirty years. They have seen the growth of the familiar European-style government octopus, along with the vanishing of the American spirit of freedom and opportunity and its replacement by a breathless search for "security" that is doomed to defeat in advance in a world where nothing, not even life itself, is secure.

Far more than the native-born, they are in a position to make comparisons. They see that America is fast becoming a nineteenth-century-model European country. They are asked to believe that this is progress. But they know from bitter experience that it just isn't so.

The American Cornerstone: Individualism

FREEDOM OF ASSEMBLY AND RELIGION, SPEECH AND PRESS stem in part from our European background. But freedom

Acknowledgment is hereby made to *Faith and Freedom,* where this article first appeared, for permission to reprint this piece here.

from government is our own American product. Let anyone who doubts this reread the American Constitution, and particularly its first ten Amendments. There he will find not merely a perfect machinery of federal government, but also a clear-cut boundary of the prerogatives of that government so far as the individual is concerned.

Our founding fathers were clearly worried about something when they added the Bill of Rights to the Constitution. The something they were worried about was not so much that the country they were endeavoring to erect would fall once more under the heel of a despot, as that it would become enslaved to government pure and simple—even government of a democratic type.

To forestall this eventuality, they set forth, in clear and unmistakable language, the basic rights of the individual with respect to government—any government. Then, with the Ninth and Tenth Amendments, they stated unequivocally that all powers not expressly delegated to the central government rest with the states or the people—in other words, with the individual, as against the collectivity.

This principle is the most basic in our Constitution, and has in the past given tone to what we choose to call our way of life. It is the fountainhead of our rugged individualism, under which we have prospered and grown great. It is what distinguishes us from other nations whose political processes are perhaps as democratic as ours, but whose outlook favors the collectivity at the expense of the individual.

It is not democracy in itself that has made us great, though it has vastly contributed to our greatness. Neither is it "liberty" in the abstract, though without liberty we could not have flourished. It is the doctrine, implied in our first ten Amendments, that the individual does not exist for the state, but the state for the individual; that the state is not the master, and the individual the servant; that the individual is endowed by God with inalienable rights, which no government can deny; that these rights do not hinge upon the whim of an autocrat, of a party in power, or even of a temporary majority of the voters, but endure by virtue of their divine origin.

These rights involve, as an inevitable corollary, certain

duties and responsibilities on the part of the individual, which he cannot shirk under penalty of putting in jeopardy his God-given rights and his American way of life.

In recent years, we have unfortunately tended to forget this basic, unique principle of our American democracy. We have tended to barter our birthright of individual freedom for a mess of pottage, looking to the central government to assume our individual burdens and responsibilities, and dole out to us in return a measure of economic security which somehow always proves to be a will-o'-the-wisp.

Today, when we are asked to voice a message of encouragement to the freedom-loving peoples of the earth who groan under Communist rule, we hesitate and pull our punches, because we know, deep down in our hearts, that we have not preserved in all its purity the heritage of individual freedom and responsibility handed down to us by the men of Valley Forge and Independence Hall. Our "Voice of America" fills the airways to Iron Curtain countries with glowing accounts of our material prosperity, but remains discreetly silent on the one main issue on which our own brand of freedom and the alleged democracy of the Communists must inevitably clash—the supreme right of the individual to order his own life free from unreasonable, stifling government restrictions, to be an individual endowed with a free soul that springs from God, and not a mindless cog in a smoothly running machine manipulated by a few masterminds who know what is best for us—or think they do.

Before America can take on the world leadership to which her material progress would seem to entitle her, she must undergo a spiritual rebirth in the faith of our founding fathers—faith in individual effort, individual achievement, individual reward.

It is no accident that the foes of our system invariably aim their first blows at religion, for all the great religions emphasize the role and importance of the individual in the eyes of God. Turn us into puppets of the state, wheels in the collectivistic machine, clods of earth with no minds or wills of our own, and you will have achieved the Socialist heaven, a heaven in which everybody dances to the same tune while the puppeteers pull the strings. And having once achieved that, we shall find ourselves back in the Middle Ages, when autocrats and oligarchies ruled, but without even the medieval comforts of a religion that proclaimed all men to be equal, at least in the eyes of God.

The system under which we of America have grown great should be described, both at home and abroad, not as capitalistic, liberal or democratic, meaningless terms in a world where state capitalism often meshes with private enterprise, where "liberal" has been distorted to accommodate Marxist fellow-travelers, and "democratic" has been appropriated by the foes of true democracy. It should be known, heralded and extolled as "individualistic."

Free Will: The Third Philosophy

THREE PHILOSOPHIES DIVIDE THE WORLD. EACH OF THEM, in the form of moral principles, political conduct and social customs, has shaped the destiny of one people or another since the dawn of recorded history. The conflict among them could go on in the future as it has gone on in the past, with one emerging triumphant in one corner of the earth, another elsewhere, save for one fact—modern technological progress, which tends to make the globe a single unit.

In the recent past it has been possible for individuals to move out from under the domination of an unwanted philosophy and go to another region where the prevailing philo-

Reprinted by permission from *Think* Magazine, Copyright 1955, by International Business Machines Corporation. Awarded in 1957 the George Washington Honor Medal by the Freedom Foundation at Valley Forge.

sophical doctrine was more in accordance with their own ideas. This becomes increasingly difficult as political units based on one or another of the three philosphies become larger and more powerful. If the time ever comes when the whole world accepts one sovereignty, escape from the prevailing philosophy will be impossible.

Accordingly, it is important for us to examine the three philosophies in detail. It is possible that the choice cannot be put off much longer.

In religion, the first of these philosophies has in the past gone by the name of predestination. In science, it is the theory of heredity. In politics, it takes many forms—divine right, aristocracy, racism. Its roots lie deep in human nature, in the selfishness and self-assertiveness that lead every one of us to think that he is just a little better than his fellowman, his ideas a little wiser, the group to which he belongs (be it family, clan, nation or race) a little superior. This is its earmark—it is never "I" who am naturally inferior; it is always "the others." And "I" am superior not by virtue of what I do, but by virtue of what I am, of what my ancestors were before me, of what God, or nature, made me.

Historically, this philosophy is exemplified by such expressions as "chosen people," "salt of the earth," "*Herrenvolk*"; and, conversely, by "pariahs," "untouchables," "*etas*," "non-Aryans." Scientifically, it is grounded in the doctrine of inherited characteristics. The foundation is none too solid, for biological heredity is modified by innumerable and obscure factors, particularly that of scientific crossings to improve breeds. Moreover, as regards man, the existence of any "pure" breed whatsoever is, at the present time, much in doubt.

Psychologically, this is the most effective belief on which a propagandist can play. "We are by nature and birthright," he says, "superior to them." And something invariably responds.

This harsh, yet all too appealing philosophy had its most recent vogue under Hitler. It is at present in fairly general disfavor, at least in the world's official circles. But let us not deceive ourselves. It has appeared too many times in the past—in the guise of "God's Elect," of slaves and masters, of "Judge Lynch," of a world divided in advance between sheep and goats, of people predestined to be saved and others predestined to be damned—to have made its final bow from the world's stage. It still springs up in the hearts of men in a stream of racial and religious intolerance as well as in the exaggerated forms of nationalism that surprisingly arise in countries that have never experienced them before. Nations like Communist China, resurgent India, newborn Indonesia, groups like the Mau Mau of Kenya and the Arab nationalists of North Africa, would not be satisfied with equality even if it were offered to them. They really aim at supremacy.

The second philosophy magnifies the importance of environment and education. It is the reverse of the first. It holds that, given the proper surroundings and upbringing, an individual can be turned into anything we want to make of him. Take slaves and the children of slaves, this doctrine asserts, give them the proper environment and education, and they will grow up to be masters. The human race can thus be reshaped by careful social planning. This is the Socialist-Communist doctrine at its purest.

But the process of change by environment and education is necessarily slow. To hasten it, a clean sweep of existing conditions must be made. But existing conditions are themselves the product of a slow process of evolution, growth, environment, education. They are deep-rooted and difficult to eradicate.

Therefore the Communists deport and destroy not as the Nazis did, to rid themselves of inferior creatures destined to remain forever inferior, but to hasten the success of their planned world. The Communists profess to believe that their victims could be reclaimed, but there is not enough time to change them. It is better that those who are hard to reclaim should disappear.

The broadening scope and influence of government in most of our Western democracies tend to encourage the growth of this philosophy even among people who are strongly individualistic by nature and tradition. Social planning here begins through individual initiative and proceeds slowly. Then, as projects become more and more ambitious, so that small groups cannot handle them, government is persuaded to take them over. They proliferate and become rigid. The fruits of this transfer of endeavor have a narcotic effect, so that people go to sleep under the illusion that government is their servant and may wake up to find that it is their master.

When the planning becomes the function of a single group of people, either in or outside the government, these people set themselves up as a superior caste. Rule is by an aristocracy of brains, and the situation differs from Communism only in degree, not in kind. Under such a system the individual ceases to exist as such and becomes part of a Plan. The characteristics that make him different from other people are not important, and tend to disappear. The Planner emerges as a superman to whom all inferior intelligences must bow. But there is evidence, in Communist states and even in the democracies, that the aristocracy of brain, in endeavoring to perpetuate itself, becomes an aristocracy of blood, or at least of a closed class. Human nature, with its inherent selfishness and egotism, triumphs again.

The third philosophy has gone in religion by the name of free will. Socially, it is known as individualism. Politically, it is libertarianism (*not* democracy, which is a method, or machinery, of governmental administration).

Under this philosophy, each individual is, within limits prescribed by the equal rights of other individuals, a law unto himself. Despite limitations of heredity, environment and education, he is nevertheless believed to be possessed of a divine spark which makes him responsible for his own actions. All men are equal before the law; all are equal in the sight of God. All are held to account for their own individual actions, and for no one else's. Their heredity does not matter; their color, race, language, nationality, religion and family are secondary; so are their respective environment and education. It is what the individual chooses to make of himself that counts.

This philosophy glorifies individual effort and initiative and upholds the individual's right to enjoy the fruits of his own labor. It allows full play for mutual help and cooperation, for projects carried out in common, for charity and social aid freely given of one's own volition. It believes in government as a moderator, co-ordinator and protector of individual activities, but not as their director.

The individual is the significant, basic unit under this philosophy. It differs from the other philosophies precisely in that it gives the individual a paramount role. In the others, the individual is supine. He receives the blessings or the curse of his heritage, or of the environment and education conferred upon him, and he acts as he is directed by forces outside of himself. But the free-willed member of an open society reacts upon his heredity and environment. He has a soul which is equal among equals, and before God.

Shall we, in our political and social thought, accept one of the two biological philosophies wherein man is a slave to his heredity or to his environment, or shall we espouse the metaphysical philosophy that makes man free, responsible, the supreme arbiter of his own destiny? The question is one on which the future may well hinge. If the world becomes one, as the signs seem to indicate, shall it be a world of free human beings or a world of regimented ants?

As we, the adherents of the philosophy of freedom and representative government, face this issue, we must be fully aware that democracy is an ongoing process under which human beings maintain themselves as free men. We must also realize that this process and spirit which have been our bulwarks of freedom could also be utilized by democracy's adherents to vote themselves into slavery.

The true answer lies in ourselves, in our own individual consciences, in our firm resolve to continue to be free individuals, even at the cost of giving up some of the material benefits which the Planners dangle before our eyes and which invariably turn out to be snares and delusions. The peasant of Russia or China who sold his birthright of individual freedom for the pottage of land reform quickly found himself a slave on a collective farm, with neither land nor freedom. The Italian or Peruvian peasant who listens to the siren song of the Communist party of his land may end the same way if he does not heed the warning of what has happened elsewhere.

We of America enjoy the inestimable advantage of having begun our life as a nation under the philosophy of free will. With us, it is not so much a question of gaining individual freedoms as of maintaining them and regaining in full those that have been encroached upon in recent years. The philosophy of freedom is one of the cornerstones of this Republic. It is our duty and our privilege to retain it for ourselves and to use it so well that we shall become a persuasive example to the rest of the world.

Why Not Turn Back?

TWO MEN WERE DRIVING ALONG AN UNFAMILIAR ROAD. They came to a fork whose branches were both marked with the same sign—the name of the town that was their destination.

The road map didn't help them. It showed only one road, approximately thirty miles to the town where they were going. The sign on the right branch agreed with the map. It, too, said thirty miles.

But the left-hand branch, not marked on their road map, looked more inviting. It was wider, straighter, better paved. Besides, its sign indicated that it was ten miles shorter. They decided to take it.

After a time, the road narrowed and the going got rough. They still went on, hoping that there would be an improvement. Instead, the road became still narrower, more filled with holes and ruts, more uncomfortable.

"Why don't we turn around, go back, and take the other road?" asked the man at the wheel.

"Oh, no! You can't turn back! We've got to go ahead!" said the other.

Half a mile farther on, the road became a veritable cow path. They slackened their speed to five miles an hour, but still they jolted and bounced. Finally, they came to a small clearing in front of a farmhouse.

"I'm going back!" said the man at the wheel, starting to turn around.

"But you can't do that!" said the other. "We're halfway down this road now. Think of all the time it will take to go back to the fork and take the other road!"

"Yes, but this car is worth something. I'm not going to wreck it. It may take longer, but we'll at least get there!"

They turned, went back to the fork, took the right-hand road, and found smooth going all the way. The experiment with the unmarked left-hand fork cost an hour of their time, but the loss was not irretrievable.

Often, in discussing political and economic matters, you hear people say: "You can't turn back the clock! You can't go backward!"

They are merely using a cliché. Ask them "Why not?" and they will be silenced.

Going ahead is an excellent practice provided you are sure you are on the right track. But what if you happen to be on the wrong one? Is it courageous to refuse to turn back? Or is it merely headstrong and foolhardy?

In political and economic affairs, we, being human, have made mistakes. We have advanced down the road to statism, smooth and easy at its outset, to the point where now the individual is about to be engulfed in the collectivistic morass, and the figure of the all-powerful state looms up before us.

Perhaps the mistakes were not obvious to everyone at the time they were made, but now they are widely recognized. What should be done about them? Should we trust reason and attempt to retrace our steps? Or should we listen to the siren voice of those who sing: "You can't turn back!"?

When the mistakes were made, many saw them in their true light. People of vision, everywhere, perceived that they were heading down the wrong road, the road that leads to the destruction of individual freedom. At the time, these farsighted people were accused of being ultra-conservative and reactionary. Today, curiously, they are accused of showing hindsight instead of being credited for foresight.

At the same time, those who made the mistakes, and those who approved of them, insist that the mistakes be compounded, that we throw good money after bad, that we continue down the road that leads nowhere rather than reverse ourselves, go back where we started, and take the right road. They say that the cure for the evils of statism is more statism, that what we really need is further encroachment of the central government upon individual rights, that the federal administration in Washington should take on more rather than fewer duties and prerogatives. They further insist that the money to carry on these manifold activities be ground out of the individual in the form of taxes, to the point where all men shall have nothing left but a mere living pittance.

The slogans of this group are familiar: "You can't go back to the horse-and-buggy days!"; "You can't turn back the wheels of progress!"; "Time marches on!"; "History does not repeat itself!"

How true are these slogans? History more often than not moves like a pendulum, and time just as often goes around in a circle. All the wheels that turn are not progress; some of them are part of screwball machinery. We have seen proof of this not only in Communist countries like the Soviet Union, China and Cuba, but in many so-called democracies run along Socialistic lines, where the last drops of lifeblood not already shed in self-defense were senselessly poured out to achieve utopian equalitarianism. We have seen it in our own country, where the "gimme" spirit has been fostered to the point where youth is robbed of its natural, God-given spirit of initiative and adventure to be imbued instead with a craving for "security" and government handouts that in the not too distant past would have been regarded as humiliating and disgraceful.

If there is something in the horse-and-buggy days worth going back to, why not go back to it? Certainly the spirit of personal initiative, personal responsibility, personal risk and reward that characterized the horse-and-buggy days is what led to our emergence as the greatest power on earth. Had it not been for the spirit of the horse-and-buggy days, there would today be no automobiles, no airplanes, no vast industrial empire in America.

All change is not necessarily beneficial, though some change undoubtedly is. What we need is to develop a sense of discrimination with respect to change. If what we changed from was better than what we changed to, there is no good reason, once the fact is established, for not discarding the new and changing back to the old.

Changes in philosophy and point of view are particularly subject to examination, revision and reversal. Such changes are usually at the base of true growth and advancement, but history shows us that they are almost as often at the root of decadence and decay. Would the fall of the Roman Empire have been possible if there had still existed, at the time when the Goths and Vandals swept in, the old spirit that had inspired the victors of the Punic Wars and the legions that under Marius cut to pieces the first wave of Germanic invaders who dared to cross the threshold of the Roman realm?

In our own specific case, America grew strong and great in the eighteenth, nineteenth and early twentieth centuries upon a philosophy of individual initiative and individual achievement, with little interference by or dependence upon a central government. To the extent that we revert to that philosophy, we shall endure strong and great. To the extent that we depart from it, to embrace the imported "isms" of a decadent Europe, bent upon following the will-o'-the-wisp of statism, in violent Communistic or milder Socialistic form, we shall make ourselves like unto our models—models which we profess not to envy, but which many in our midst nevertheless secretly or openly wish to imitate.

The evil results of certain changes made within the last half century in our political, economic and social structure are self-evident today. They appear in our philosophy of government taxing and government spending, in our foreign policy, in the gradual submersion of the individual by the state, in the dependence of large segments of our population upon government bounty, in the fuzzy thinking that pervades many of our educational institutions. A return to some of the older outlooks and principles, upon which our country grew great, seems to be in order.

This emphatically does not mean that we must discard real improvements, or stop seeking better ways to do things. All it means is that we must retain what has been proved right and get rid of what has been proved wrong.

Fear of Government

SHOULD OUR PERSONAL PHILOSOPHY TOWARD GOVERNment include an element of fear? To a generation brought up in the last thirty years, during which many have been trained to look to government for all material blessings, the question may sound strange.

"Are we not identical with the government?" they will ask. "In a country democratically run, where the executive and lawmakers are chosen by the people, what danger can there be in government?"

What is too often forgotten is that the best of elected executives and lawgivers are, like the rest of us, fallible human beings and subject to normal human temptations and errors. The worst may be potential autocrats and dictators.

The democratic process is, unfortunately, in itself no secure guarantee against the emergence of authoritarianism. Both Mussolini and Hitler came to power through a succession of constitutional and democratic processes and measures. In many of the countries that now find themselves behind the Iron Curtain the same methods were employed. The Czech Communists, like the Italian Fascists and the German Nazis before them, began by polling a sizable vote which was, however, far short of a majority. By combining with weak-minded parties of the right or left, they formed in each instance a coalition which was able to gain control of the government. Then came the gradual "purification," whereby the former political allies were absorbed or cast aside, until the revolutionary minority held absolute power.

In two-party countries such as ours, it would not even be necessary for a party to go through the coalition stage. By wielding effective control over the executive, legislative and judicial branches of the government, it could, as the result of a thoroughly democratic process, deprive us of our liberties.

Hence, eternal vigilance on the part of the people is truly the price of liberty. Aggressive, freedom-destroying tendencies on the part of government (which, in effect, means the party in power) must be corrected by the ballot box before it is too late.

Our system of government, thanks to the Constitution, is as nearly perfect an instrument for the preservation of our freedoms as a man-made piece of political machinery can be. Yet it must not be forgotten that it carries the seed of its own undoing if a leader, or a party, succeeds in rolling up sufficient majorities for its modification or even its abolition. Leaders, parties and majorities are human, therefore fallible, and history shows that individual liberties are easily lost, but not at all easily regained. Add to this the possible tendency, on the part of a non-elective judiciary, to interpret the Constitution in such a way as to distort or nullify it.

Many of our younger people, nurtured in the government paternalism fostered by the New and Fair Deals, the New Frontier and the Great Society, find it difficult to believe that any government, chosen by themselves, could be anything but an instrument for public progress and the common welfare. To such a government they are willing to surrender their God-given right of initiative and self-determination in exchange for the benefits and security the government offers. Theirs is an illusion. The benefits and security can be no greater than they could themselves accumulate by their own unhampered efforts, while the danger that such a government may in its Socialistic course reach a point of no return is ever-present.

For every benefit that the government holds out, the question should be asked: "What am I required to give up in return?" A careful formulation of an answer will usually bring to light that the price demanded is greater than the benefit offered—whether in taxes, or in restriction of individual freedom and initiative, or in self-respect.

We should love our government insofar as it is an expression of the will of the people. We should fear it, as Frankenstein should have feared his creation, for the monster it may turn into under given conditions. It is not so much the function of government to control the people as it is the function of the people to control their government.

Freedom: A Science Or An Emotion?

A EUROPEAN POLITICAL LEADER ONCE SAID THAT THERE was urgent need for revising our thinking about freedom; that it had too long been treated as an emotion, and made to serve all sorts of purposes, including those diametrically opposite to any conceivable theory based upon the etymological meaning of the word; that it was high time to begin to study freedom as a science, with carefully drawn definitions and boundaries, outlining on a basis acceptable to all honest men what freedom is and how far it goes.

As a matter of fact, there is no word that has lent itself to greater fluctuations of interpretation and distortions of meaning than "freedom," or its synonym, "liberty." To cite some extreme examples of distortion, references to the word appear in the Nazi *Horst Wessel* song, in the Fascist hymn *Giovinezza,* in the national anthem of the Soviets. The first states at one point: "The day for freedom and bread is dawning"; the second says: "In Fascism is the salvation of our liberty"; the third includes the words: "Mighty Russia has forged an inviolable union of free Republics."

Without necessarily accusing the songwriters of hypocrisy, one could point to the widely different points of view that these lines imply. The Nazi writer, linking freedom with bread, points to what our own FDR would have called "freedom from want," a highly negative form of freedom, and one calling for a passive rather than an active attitude. The Fascist writer, forgetting about the frying pan and the fire, was probably thinking of the Communist excesses that in Italy preceded the March on Rome, and the fact that without Mussolini's seizure of power the country would have succumbed to Communist enslavement. The Russian writer speaks of "free" Republics in the customary Communist acceptance: freedom within the collectivistic orbit, cultural autonomy coupled with economic and personal servitude to an all-powerful state representing, at least in theory, the collectivity.

It has often been pointed out that freedom is a highly relative term. In the freest democracy in the world, I still am not free to drive a car at ninety miles an hour down the main street; the freedom of others to live takes precedence over my freedom to drive any way I please. Someone once said jocularly that my freedom to swing my arm ends where the tip of his nose begins. Freedom must be subordinated to law and order, and law and order must take into account the freedom of all men, not just of some.

But when all factors are taken into account and all allowances made, it is still evident that some freedoms are basic, while other so-called freedoms are not. Of Roosevelt's Four Freedoms, freedom of speech and of the press is basic, even if circumscribed by libel and antisedition laws. Freedom of worship is even more basic, and upon it no restrictions should be placed save in those extreme and rare cases where a religious belief involves harm to others. Freedom from want and freedom from fear are far from basic. "Want," in one sense of the word, is what makes the world go round. If human beings did not want, there would be no progress; in fact, there would be no human beings. If by want is meant poverty, there is still the same objection. Extreme poverty is an evil, but not an undiluted one. The person who feels poor in this world's goods has an incentive to go out and seek remedies, and this in turn leads to progress and self-improvement. Freedom from fear, in its bald form, is sheer nonsense, for we live in an existence where fear is not only natural and unavoidable, but desirable. Fear is the basic ingredient in the instinct of self-preservation, without which we would all perish. If we seek freedom from fear of something or other, then it all depends on what we fear. Fear of the loss of a livelihood is what makes some people work. Fear of God, or of the law, is what keeps others from committing crime. It is possible that FDR had in mind fear of religious or racial persecution, in which case his fourth freedom is justified, save that a few other justifiable fears might be added, such as fear of loss of freedom itself through excessive government, or of persecution by agencies of that government.

That liberty and freedom are used as convenient slogans more often than any other words, with the possible exception of God, country and family, will scarcely be disputed by anyone. But precisely what is liberty, and what is freedom? The numerous dictionary definitions help us very little. Perhaps the best is "the ability or capacity to act without undue hindrance or restriction." But even this begs the question; what is "undue"?

The current civil rights controversy has focused attention on the definition of freedom and liberty perhaps to a greater extent than any other recent event. Here some of the claims of civil rights advocates were accepted without discussion by an overwhelming majority of people who were not blinded by prejudice or tradition; others were of such a nature as to arouse serious controversy, even in areas where enforced segregation had long ceased to exist. Such principles as "racial imbalance," quota systems for employment regardless of merit or fitness, compensation for past wrongs not committed by the present-day community, somehow go against the grain, or, better yet, against our innate sense of justice. Yet these principles were just as much defended on grounds of "freedom" as were the most stringent and humiliating segregationist practices of certain areas.

To an even greater degree, the civil rights and Vietnam controversies have carried to the fore other thorny aspects of freedom previously brought into relief by labor unions. Is one's freedom to demonstrate peaceably and publicly air one's grievances superior to the freedom of another not to have his legitimate pursuits interfered with? Which is the more basic freedom, that of the obstructive picket line or that of the person who wishes to cross it? Should there be freedom to interfere with lawful means of transportation and transit, and disrupt a city's traffic? At what point does the right of assembly and petition for redress end, and disorderly conduct begin? Which ranks higher, the freedom to live where one pleases, or the freedom to dispose of one's property in any way one pleases? Does freedom to organize take precedence over freedom to work? These are not idle questions, and whatever ultraliberals (or, for that matter, ultraconservatives) may say, there are two possible answers.

We might be tempted to leave the interpretation of what is and what is not freedom to the courts of law, but the decisions of the courts are too often inspired by political motives and the expediency of the moment, as illustrated by the spectacular reversals in the judgments of our own Supreme Court.

Perhaps in the final analysis the best definition of freedom is what springs from the individual conscience of reasoning and decent human beings. It is true that the law forbids me to engage in certain acts of "freedom"; but it is equally true that in the commission of those acts I would run foul of my own conscience. It is no accident that certain laws are almost universally respected and observed, save by an out-and-out criminal element definitely known to be such and correspondingly condemned by the entire community, while others are the object of widespread violation and contempt. Where statute law does not coincide with moral law, there is trouble.

The moral law at its purest is best expressed in the Ten Commandments. Beyond that, there are laws that correspond to a generally acknowledged social expediency, and are accepted by the majority. Lastly, there are laws which embody someone's convenience or profit to someone else's detriment, and for which there is only legal, not moral, justification. Yet all these laws, good, bad and indifferent, enter into our concept of freedom.

It would not be amiss occasionally to review and revise our body of laws and concepts, and certainly it is not amiss to re-examine and question some of them. To the extent that we can make our laws and concepts of freedom coincide with the moral sense of the community, or with what we might term the mass conscience, those laws and concepts will have a better chance of being observed and enforced.

A scientific study of freedom, as opposed to the emotional treatment which freedom almost invariably gets, would start by taking into account the moral law and the overwhelming consensus of the mass conscience. It could then go on to examine the debatable areas, and attempt to determine which angles of freedom are more fundamental, and which are based upon tradition and custom that today have become largely obsolete and meaningless. Last of all, there would be the most difficult task of establishing clear-cut boundaries between one freedom and another. Almost inevitably, and despite all conscientious efforts, there would be a residue of highly debatable cases in which two freedoms clash; these would have to be solved by reasonable compromise.

In this process of scientific examination of freedom, the moral sense and moral conscience would be uppermost. The greatest mistake that lawmakers can commit is to set up a law (or a definition of freedom), and then attempt to reshape the moral sense and the mass and individual conscience on the basis of what they have set up. This procedure has been tried and found wanting so many times that one cannot avoid the conclusion that it is hopelessly unscientific.

The Constitution and the Supreme Court

THOSE WHO BELIEVE THAT MORALITY CAN BE LEGISLATED urge us to accept and respect the recent decisions of the Supreme Court regarding integration and prayer in the schools.

For what concerns mechanical observance, they are right. While it stands, the law of the land must be respected, observed and enforced, or all respect for all law will cease, and we shall be plunged into anarchy. It is the function of the courts to interpret the laws, and the function of the Supreme Court to interpret the Constitution.

But this emphatically does not mean that we must hold these or other Supreme Court decisions sacred, and not work actively for their reversal if they don't agree with our individual moral conscience. A Court decision is legally, but not morally, binding.

Above all, it is not, like the decrees of the Medes and the Persians, irreversible. If it were, we would still be living by the Dred Scott Decision and the Fugitive Slave Law. Slavery and its evils would still be with us.

We can recall Roosevelt's angry rantings about the "Nine Old Men," and his attempt to pack the Supreme Court in the same fashion that Queen Victoria threatened to pack the House of Lords if it didn't subscribe to measures approved by the House of Commons. These are only two of the glaring occasions when the "liberal"-minded did not hesitate to exercise their own judgment, regardless of the sanctity of traditional institutions.

The Supreme Court is composed of men. These men do not even have the merit of being elected by the people, as are the President and the members of Congress. They may be eminent jurists, and highly versed in the laws of the land, but there is no clear provision to that effect. They are presidential appointees, and naturally tend to reflect the attitude and point of view of the man who selected them. Their selection is in some cases inspired by political considerations. Some appointments have even been in the nature of payment for political debts contracted at national conventions.

After a succession of conservative Presidents (Harding, Coolidge, Hoover), the Supreme Court tends to be conservative. After a succession of liberal Presidents (Roosevelt, Truman, Eisenhower, Kennedy, Johnson), the Supreme Court tends to be liberal. It is not necessary to impugn the honesty or sincerity of the Justices to assert that their interpretation of the Constitution is colored by their own thinking. Few of us can rise sufficiently above the subjective level to render a decision that runs altogether counter to our views.

Many of us happen to think that in interfering with the schools, both on the issue of integration and that of prayer, the Supreme Court was stepping out of bounds. This has nothing to do with the merits of either integration or prayer. It is merely a question of constitutional procedure.

The Constitution says nothing whatsoever about schools or education. It does expressly state that all powers not specifically conferred upon the Federal Government are reserved to the states and the people. This includes, or should include, control over the schools.

If precedent and custom mean anything, they are on the side of states' rights in this instance. The states have always run and paid for their own educational systems. Until very recently, the Federal Government did not even have a federal bureau, let alone a department of education. It is of interest to note that when the latter was created, the Federal Government did not have enough confidence in its right to do so to let it stand on its own feet. It found it expedient to couple education with health and public welfare to justify its new activity, even in its own eyes.

I do not say that the Federal Government should not exercise complete or concurrent power over education, which is a far more complex thing today than it was in the days of the founding fathers. Many democratic countries that we admire have public education systems run by the central government, and no irreparable harm seems to result.

Neither do I say that schools should not be integrated. In fact, I would say the opposite, for racial segregation strikes me as basically unfair and contrary to both American and Christian principles, in which I believe, though I admit there may be temporary or local justification for some measure of gradualism in correcting the evil.

But I do hold that the proper way to effect such a radical transfer of power from the states and the people to the Federal Government is through the clearly outlined process of constitutional amendment, not through Court decision. In interpreting the Constitution, the Supreme Court does not have the right to annul it. And annulment, to my mind at least, is precisely what results from its decision to put the Federal Government into a field from which the Constitution excludes it.

Prayer in the schools goes even further. Here the basis for Supreme Court interference is the Constitution's prohibition to create an established religion. But the simple acknowledgment of the existence of God and our dependence on Him does not establish any religion. Nonbelievers in God can and should be excused, to safeguard their freedom of conscience. But they should not try to deprive the rest of us of ours, on the specious pretext that it stunts their psychological growth to have to leave the classroom while the prayer is in progress.

The logical corollary to the prohibition of prayer in the schools on grounds of an established religion is the abolition of the use of the Bible and the name of God in all the oaths of office and all the courts of law, along with the erasing of any reference to God in our coinage and seals. If we are going to turn ourselves into an officially Godless society, we should have the courage to do a thorough job, as the Soviet Union has done, and not leave the issue hanging in the air.

The Supreme Court has reversed itself before. It may do so again. Meanwhile, our only obligation is to observe its decisions, not necessarily to approve them or even respect them, save in compliance.

We can hasten the day of reversal. We can even force it, by the same process of constitutional amendment that the Federal Government ought to invoke as often as it feels the need of extending its authority and functions. A court of review composed of the chief justices of the fifty states might give us a more balanced picture, and be more in accord with the true will of the people, which is, after all, the basis of our system of government.

Government by Pressure Groups

DIVIDE ET IMPERA! "DIVIDE AND RULE!" THIS USED TO be the motto of the old Hapsburg Empire, where no fewer than twelve different nationalities were held together under one single bond of personal fealty to the Crown. By setting off one group against another, cunningly playing upon their racial and cultural antipathies, the Hapsburgs managed to endure for a thousand years.

But the game of divide and conquer could be played once too often. When the Austro-Hungarian armies suffered a crushing defeat at the hands of Italy in World War One, the empire with its deep-seated, government-fostered divisions, collapsed and crumbled like a house of cards. Wilson's principle of self-determination for small nations, irrespective of economic realities, took over, to the ultimate detriment of the new small nations that had emerged from the wreckage of the Hapsburg Empire; but it took another world war and the triumph of Communism in eastern Europe to bring that about.

America, since its inception, has been composed of different groups, with variegated racial, cultural and religious backgrounds. Emphasis, however, was on American unity. Immigrants to this country were actively encouraged to become citizens and assimilate themselves to the preexisting American citizenry. The official language was English, save in New Mexico, where Spanish was co-official by reason of a large Mexican population that antedated annexation and statehood. The official body of law was English common law, save in Louisiana, where the Napoleonic Code was used in deference to a large preexisting French population. There was, happily, no official religion.

There were on American soil different racial groups, composed for the most part of first-generation immigrants who remained only partly assimilated to the day they died. But their American-born children normally lost their ancestral identity and merged with the great body of Americans, with only their names and perhaps a preference for certain foods to distinguish them from other Americans.

To the best of this writer's knowledge, Mrs. Eleanor Roosevelt was the first to apply the term "racial minorities" to American groups of non-Anglo-Saxon background and ancestry. This aroused a storm of protest from other columnists, who were quick to point out that one could not confuse the American groups, resulting from voluntary immigration to this country, with minority groups in European countries, having their roots in the lands in which they lived, even though not forming part of the numerically or politically dominant group. The hyphenate groups of America, it was argued, had come here of their own free will, under an unwritten contract to accept the customs, laws, institutions and language of the host nation; therefore their rights as separate, individual group entities were nonexistent, even while their rights as newly assimilated American citizens gave them parity with the native-born.

An earlier Roosevelt, Theodore, had at one time spoken out in no uncertain terms against what he called the undesirable "boardinghouse" concept of America, as a land where each newly arrived group could continue to use its own language and customs and reject assimilation by the preexisting majority. But even in his days, perhaps even more than in those of Mrs. Roosevelt, there were Little Italys and Chinatowns, Polish sections and Irish ones, and there were even well-defined voting blocs, organized by the various big-city Tammany Halls. The main difference lay perhaps in the attitude of the dominant group. While Theodore decried and deplored the existence of a separatist mentality, Eleanor gave it official recognition and encouragement.

It would be easy enough to accept the reality of cultural diversity, particularly in the first or immigrant generation, along with the assurance that this cultural diversity tends to disappear as soon as American-born generations come on the scene. Cultural diversity is an enrichment rather than an impoverishment, since it makes available to the American population as a whole the very real achievements in civilization of each separate group. This is the true meaning of "melting pot," a term of which we were once rather proud.

Opposed to the melting-pot concept is the political exploitation of racial diversity, the tendency of politicians to organize cultural, racial, religious and other groups into voting blocs that will think not along lines of what is best for America, but of what is best for the group, or, worse yet, for the interests of the country where the racial bloc originated. Blood is thicker than water, and it is fairly natural that an American Jew should favor the Israeli viewpoint over the Arab, or the American of Irish extraction the claim of the Irish Republic to the six northern counties. But all too often, local as well as international issues tend to be judged on a minority group basis.

By reason of the constitutional provision that the electoral college in presidential elections shall go by state units rather than in proportion to the popular vote in each state, or according to the popular vote in the nation at large, we have a peculiar domination of the American political scene by Mrs. Roosevelt's minority groups. In closely contested states with large blocs of electoral votes, it is not at all unusual for the state and all its electors to be won or lost by a party or a candidate on the basis of a shift of a few thousand or even a few hundred out of millions of votes. This confers upon organized minority groups and their leaders and spokesmen a power which is altogether out of proportion to their real numerical importance, and which can only be described as a form of blackmail.

"Give us what we want," say the Negro leaders (or the Jewish, or Irish, or Italian, or Polish, or Puerto Rican leaders), "or we'll swing our bloc of votes over to the other side, and cause you to lose the entire electoral vote of New York State (or Illinois, or Ohio, or Massachusetts)." Faced with this threat, politicians, whose sole concern is to gain and hold office, bend over backward to satisfy the demands, reasonable or otherwise, of the minorities. The majority, under these circumstances, is often forgotten, or at least neglected. It is figured that non-minority voters will distribute themselves along party lines or vote traditionally, anyway. What matters is to get on your side that bloc of a hundred thousand out of four million votes that may spell the difference between winning or losing the state's electoral vote.

The pressure-group game can, of course, be played by other than racial groups. Labor union leaders make frequent threats of political reprisals and promises of political support. Even religious denominations have been known to play.

That there is a basis of reality in the pressure-group vote is undoubted. Its extent, and the effective control exercised by "leaders" over the voting of the group they claim to represent, is something else. There have been spectacular cases where candidates have won spanking majorities in the face of minority group threats. Robert A. Taft at one time swept Ohio by a half million vote majority over the opposition of organized labor. There have also been cases where a dormant majority was finally aroused out of its slumber by the threat of minority domination and set out to prove that the nonaffiliated voter cannot be altogether left out of a politician's calculations. There are also those cases where two parties cancel each other out by kowtowing to the vociferous minority to approximately the same extent. What choice, for example, does a Negro or Puerto Rican bloc in New York City have as between Rockefeller and Kennedy? Both favor civil rights and kid-glove treatment for the dominant minorities. By the same token, what chance does the unaffiliated voter have of registering his protest against policies that have the local support of both major parties?

Little if any remedy exists for the pressure-group situation in purely local, or even statewide elections. The crux of the matter comes in the presidential election, which is nationwide, but on a state-by-state basis, with winner-take-all in each individual state. Here the remedy lies not so much in putting the election on a nationwide popular majority basis, since it is still desirable to preserve the individuality of the states in a national election, but in splitting up the electors from each state in proportion to the popular vote in that state.

This would preserve the principle of states' rights in a national election, and have the added advantage of giving some measure of proportional representation to splinter parties, which sometimes represent sizable segments of public opinion.

But above all, it would tend to cut down to size the importance of minority groups and voting blocs, which is now entirely out of proportion to the real size and importance of those groups and blocs. A bloc of fewer than a hundred thousand voters would then no longer be in a position to threaten the two great national parties with the loss of the total electoral vote of the big industrial states, though it could still claim to be able to swing the vote of two or three electors, as is just and proper.

Of all the needed amendments to the Constitution, this is perhaps one of the most vital if true democracy and political equality for all voters are to be preserved.

A Reply To Henry Steele Commager

(*Early in July, 1963, there appeared in* The New York Times Magazine *an article by Professor Henry Steele Commager upholding the Federal Government as the champion of human and civil rights against the encroachments of the states. This brief note of comment, sent to and received by the* Times *editor, was not published. It is hereby expressly acknowledged that the* Times, *as a privately owned newspaper with its own editorial policy, was altogether within its rights in not publishing the letter.*)

IN HIS IMPASSIONED DEFENSE OF A FEDERAL GOVERNMENT that can do no wrong, and his equally virulent attack upon the states, Professor Commager overlooks the all-important point that both the federal and the local governments vie in encroaching upon the rights of the individual, for whom all our constitutional guarantees were set up.

When the Federal Government imposes confiscatory income and estate taxes upon the individual, and its lead is followed by the states and even by municipalities, there is an infringement of the individual's rights to enjoy the fruits of his own labor, and consequently of his right to the pursuit of happiness. It has been abundantly proved that exorbitant and steeply graduated tax rates are designed not to raise needed revenue, but to accomplish a social purpose—the redistribution of income and wealth, in accordance with a formula once propounded by Lenin. The result is visible in our weakened moral fiber, padded expense accounts and deductions, and far too numerous and influential tax-exempt foundations. In addition, the personal income tax, whether federal or state, gives the government the power to meddle in the private affairs of the individual, and thus deprives him of his liberty.

Prohibition, one of the greatest violations of individual rights on record, was initiated by states and localities; but it was picked up by the Federal Government and made the object of a noble social experiment that ended ingloriously after having made us the laughingstock of the world and regaled us with the bootlegger, the speakeasy and the gang war.

A federal social security law that says that an individual, after having contributed all his life, shall be deprived of his benefits if he continues to work at 65, places undue and unreasonable restrictions upon individual freedom.

A federal or local government that prescribes minimum wages is not only infringing upon the right of the individual to bargain freely; it is also restricting employment and eliminating jobs that might otherwise be freely contracted for and filled at lower rates.

When the Supreme Court tells the individual states how to run their educational systems, it is out of bounds. Education, by the terms of the Constitution, is a function reserved to the states and the people. If we want that changed (and we may), let us pass a constitutional amendment to that effect. Instead, the Supreme Court even takes it upon itself to tell the states whether there shall be prayer in the schools which the states are paying for.

When a state, southern or northern (yes, there are several northern ones), passes laws forbidding people of different races to marry or mingle as they please, it is violating the rights of the individual. When a northern state, or the Federal Government, passes laws forcing people to mingle against their will, it is equally at fault. A southern state that denies its public educational facilities to duly qualified students by reason of race or color is stepping heavily on the rights of man. A northern state or locality that prescribes that schoolchildren shall be forcibly lifted out of their own neighborhood school and natural environment so that they may be "integrated," and racial "imbalance" corrected, is doing just as badly.

It is an infringement of individual freedom to prescribe that one shall not live in a certain area on account of his race or color. It is equally an infringement to prescribe that a private individual shall not freely buy from or sell or rent his property to whom he pleases, whatever his motives.

Let us beware lest misinterpreted welfare clauses and civil rights deprive us of our older civil liberties, and reduce us to the status of a totalitarian nation.

The Menace of the Bureaucratic Mind

"WITH A STUBBORNNESS AND ARROGANCE CHARACTERISTIC of the bureaucratic mind, it [the State Department] still insists on the right to decide what is best for the United States."

The above words are not mine, nor are they spoken by any conservative. They appear in an article by Henry Steele Commager, writing in *The New York Times Magazine* (October 20, 1963, page 109), which deals with the State Department's refusal to issue passports to certain American citizens.

There are roughly, at the present time, two and a half million civilian federal employees. There are close to three million people in or connected with the armed forces. The number of state and municipal employees has been estimated by Chase Manhattan Bank statisticians at seven million. This gives us, very roughly, 13.5 percent of the working population in some form of government employment, exclusive of the military. The same statisticians further figure, on the basis of present trends, that by 1970 there will be one government employee for every five in private industry, and one for every four in 1980.

How many million workers are employed by private industries engaged in government projects is anybody's guess. Five million is probably a conservative estimate. One source of information claims that 70 percent of our scientific talent works, directly or indirectly, for the government, leaving only 30 percent for private industrial development.

All this may be bad from an economic point of view, but you can't prove it. In Communist countries practically every worker works for the government, and those countries haven't gone on the rocks yet. Also, there is a school of economics that claims that it isn't who gets income, or for what, that counts, but how fast that income circulates. This also may be true, in which case government spending, even of the boondoggling variety, would be economically justified.

But there is one thing connected with expanding government bureaus that gives one pause and lends itself to certain considerations. The government bureaucrat, if he plies his trade long enough, thinks he has a vested interest in it. He feels, by virtue of his position, slightly superior to the rest of the population, since he can in some measure control their activities and force his point of view upon them. In certain respects, he rules the roost. Next, he acquires an exaggerated sense of importance: his own and that of his activities. Instead of placing the latter in proper perspective with relation to the total activities of the nation, or even of the government, he considers them paramount. This leads to a desire to increase the scope and range of those activities, and add to the number of people working under his orders. The ultimate result is bureaucratic empire-building.

Note that in behaving as he does, the bureaucrat is acting as a perfectly normal human being. It is natural for us to be self-centered, to consider our activities paramount, to wish to influence and control other people. The bureaucrat normally believes in the importance of what he is doing. He is thoroughly honest, according to his lights.

But without questioning the sincerity of his motives, we may legitimately consider how his behavior affects the rest of us. Government bureaus and government activities, federal, state and local, have been proliferating and expanding at an unbelievable rate in the course of the last thirty years. The rate of their expansion is accelerating. If it continues to gain momentum in the next thirty years as it has in the past, the end of the century will see government in full control of everything. We shall have achieved the Socialist heaven, and Khrushchev will have buried us, so far as our economic and political system is concerned. It is as simple as that, and we may as well look the facts in the face.

There are many among us who profess to think this is a desirable outcome. While they deplore Communism with their lips, in their hearts they favor its basic tenet: "government ownership and operation of the means of production," with the corollary "full government control over the individual and his activities."

This runs counter to the doctrine of individualism. It runs counter to the belief in personal freedom. It runs counter to the principles on which this nation was built, and to the Constitution that embodies those principles.

If this is what we want, let us have it. But let us have it with our eyes open, knowing precisely what we are doing, not under the influence of a narcotic that causes a song of freedom to ring in our ears at the same time that chains are being riveted around our wrists and ankles.

The bureaucrat, sincere or otherwise, is a relentless empire-builder. Many new bureaus, functions, activities of government, federal, state and local, come into being every day, calling for new taxes, new forms to fill out, new restrictions for the individual and for legitimate business, new headaches and impediments of all sorts for private enterprise and individual endeavor.

How many bureaus, functions and activities of government, federal, state or local, disappear? Few, if any. It is a never-ending source of wonderment to see how many tasks for which there is no longer either use or justification are retained because the bureaucrats in charge refuse to relinquish them. The number of government bureaus and government activities which arose out of an "emergency" is legion. When the emergency is long since past, the bureau lives on. To cite just one well-known instance: the farm price support program was enacted to encourage farm production at a time when it was desperately needed. It lives on, at a cost of over seven billion dollars a year, to plague farmers, consumers and taxpayers alike, raise everybody's living costs, preclude our competing in world markets. There are said to be well over a hundred thousand Department of Agriculture workers throughout the country, one for every sixty persons engaged in agriculture.

On the local level, the New York City sales tax, recently raised to 4 percent, was originally enacted during the Great Depression as a 1 percent tax "for the relief of unemployment." Its revenues are now used for the relief of anybody who cares to apply. Yet unemployment of the Great Depression type has been over since 1940. The bureaucrats who administer both sales tax and relief would be more than horrified if anyone were to suggest that either be discontinued. Rent control laws, which led to the slummification of vast areas of our major cities by making it impossible for landlords to render the services they had previously rendered to their tenants, are still widespread.

Consider the penetration of both federal and state governments into local matters that should be the concern of the individual locality, the duplication and triplication of functions that could be more efficiently performed by a single agency, of taxes that could be more efficiently collected by a single government. More bureaus, more government employees, more restrictions and obligations upon the individual, who is caught in the tentacles of a tripartite government octopus. Federal laws, state laws, local ordinances and regulations, often contradictory and conflicting. Paper work, reports and questionnaires, storing of records. Waste of valuable time and labor that could be devoted to productive uses.

Episodes are of little moment, and everyone has his own episodes to narrate, from the man who followed the advice of his local Internal Revenue office in respect to a certain deduction and later found himself assessed penalties and fines, in addition to having his deduction disallowed, to the housewife who got in trouble because she neglected to perform the triple operation of withholding federal, state and Social Security taxes for the maid who came to do her housework once a week. My own favorite experience is in connection with limited earnings during a three-month stay in the state of California in 1960. There is seemingly no state withholding there, and no one bothered to inform me of the existence of a state income tax. It took three years for California to catch up with me back in the East, but they finally did. One might expect that having found out about my earnings, they would figure out how much, if anything, I owed them, and bill me for the amount. Not at all. They asked me to figure it out, on the basis of a complicated formula. It turned out that having paid a much stiffer state income tax on my California earnings to the state of New York, of which I was a resident, I owed California nothing. It took six months of correspondence to establish this fact. The joke? Had I not paid income tax to New York, I would have owed California exactly $2.50, a sum I would have gladly paid for the privilege of spending three months in that beautiful state, if they had simply sent me a bill for the amount. I hate to think what it must have cost the California taxpayers to try to collect that $2.50 which they didn't even get.

But why blame the lowly California bureaucrats? They were only trying to do their duty as they saw it, and in accordance with their regulations.

Of far greater moment is the menace of the bureaucratic mind in its higher echelons, the ones that construct empires for which there is dubious justification, expand them when they should be cut down, maintain them when their usefulness is long past.

The population at large is often regaled with propaganda from these people. They present their activities as highly useful and deserving of expansion. "For a cost of only two billion dollars a year," they tell us, "which is less than the people of the United States spend on movies, or candy, or cosmetics, or liquor, or tobacco, we could have——" What we could have ranges all the way from expanded educational and welfare facilities at home (and these would, in the words of their sponsors, abolish illiteracy, school dropouts, juvenile delinquency, old-age poverty, the need for medical care, etc., etc., etc.) to the love, gratitude and admiration of the outside world, particularly those uncommitted backward nations that don't care whether they get their handouts from Washington or Moscow.

All we would have to do is set up a new federal bureau, heavily staffed with the usual functionaries, and put it into operation, at a cost lower than what we spend on one or another of our vices or non-necessities.

The trouble with these well-meaning projects is that they run into the dozens, not to say the hundreds. Multiply "only two billion dollars" by fifty, and you have doubled the federal budget. Also, federal taxation.

It is quite possible that we might be better off without liquor, candy or tobacco, movies or cosmetics. But aside from the squawk that would arise from the portion of our population that likes and uses those products, they are at least self-liquidating, and bring in revenue. The advantages of the substitutes urged by do-gooding bureaucrats are invisible, intangible, and often quite hypothetical.

The visionary bureaucratic type of mind is a menace only to the extent that it succeeds in capturing the attention of Congress or the state legislatures, which unfortunately it does all too often.

The practical bureaucrat is the one who already has his bureau and proceeds to expand it and its activities by executive fiat. Bureau budgets always go up, never down. Long before Parkinson's Laws were formulated, we knew that a bureau's work can be expanded to meet any and all increased appropriations. If the appropriation is there and the work is not, the work can very easily be created.

This does not mean that the bureaucratic force is hired to sit on its hands. The amount of work actually performed by a bureaucrat, the amount of time he puts into it, the amount of mental and occasionally physical effort involved, compare not unfavorably with what goes on in private, productive industry. The Depression showed us that the man who raked leaves or cut down trees on a PWA project could break his back just as effectively as the one who harvested wheat.

The difference lies in the outcome of these activities. Private industry has a very effective means of checking on the effectiveness of its activities—profits and losses. Government bureaus, save in a few isolated cases, do not have this check.

Whether a government operation is beneficial or not to the community as a whole is all too often a matter of conjecture and controversy. The bureaucrat in charge, and most of his underlings, will naturally claim that it is highly beneficial. Why should they cut their own throats? Besides, many of them are genuinely convinced of the worthiness of what they are doing.

It is possible that the taxpayer, if he gives the matter any thought, may be equally prejudiced. If he is an educated, and not a blind taxpayer, he will view the operation from the standpoint of what it costs him and what benefits he derives from it. But educated taxpayers are the exception. The bureaucrat is too often the "expert" in the field. Far too often he has his way.

One unpleasant facet of the bureaucratic mind is the growing arrogance of some (by no means all) bureaucrats. In past history, the bureaucrat was appointed by the king, who ruled by divine right and could do no wrong. It was therefore natural for the bureaucrat to look down upon the taxpayer, whom he viewed, more often than not, as a necessary evil, and to whom he owed no allegiance.

In a Western-type modern democracy, the bureaucrat, no matter how or by whom appointed, is a servant of the people, at least in theory. His relationship to the taxpayer, who in effect pays his salary, should be that of a producer to his customer. It is perhaps an exaggeration to say that the customer is always right; but there should be a good deal of consideration paid the customer by the producer, and, correspondingly, by the bureaucrat to the taxpayer.

Some (not all) bureaucrats tend to forget this, and behave as though they were royal appointees in a medieval state. They entrench themselves behind the laws or the bureau directives. Again, there are episodes which do not prove too much, save the existence of a state of mind.

There was, for instance, the use of New York State's antitrust law by the office of the Attorney General as the basis for subpoenas in alleged discrimination cases. No other law applied at the time, but the theory used was to the effect that discrimination restrains business. Regardless of how one may feel about discrimination, this contention holds no water, and should have been thrown out by the courts. Its value here is that it tends to throw some light on the tendency of some bureaucrats to behave like czars and impose their point of view by hook or crook.

It may be stressed that none of these phenomena are new. Least new of all is the bureaucratic mind, as we have attempted to describe it.

The remedy for its abuses does not lie in specific protests or proceedings against any one man, or any one bureau. It lies in vigilance and watchfulness on the part of an enlightened citizenry against the encroachments of the bureaucratic mind, in the enforcement of civil liberties and constitutional rights against the governmental juggernaut, on any level.

Above all, it lies in circumscribing bureaucratic activities, and in the reduction in numbers and powers of existing bureaucracies. "Is this bureau really necessary?" should be the slogan. If it is not, let us have the courage to demand its abolition. If it is, let us see to it that it limits itself to the function for which it was created.

In accordance with the spirit of the Constitution, the Federal Government should do nothing which can more properly be done by the states; the states should do nothing which can more properly be done by the localities; the localities should do nothing which can safely be left to the discretion of the individual citizen.

Why Not Try Democracy?

"DEMOCRACY" IS A LOVELY CATCHWORD. ETYMOLOGICALLY, it means "people's rule," or "people's government." In theory, the people make their wishes known through their elected representatives, and those wishes are carried out.

The trouble with democracy is the same as the trouble with Christianity. It has never really been tried out, despite all the lip service paid to it.

The people are seldom consulted on any specific issue, or even on broad questions of principle or policy. Once a year, the people are given a choice between two or more opposing slates of candidates for office. The candidates and the parties they belong to give pledges which are sometimes even kept. But the pledges, too, come in the form of a slate. While I, as an individual, or the majority of the voters, may favor a certain number of pledges in a given platform, we may oppose certain others. All we can do as voters is to take a general cross-section of pledges and issues, and vote for the candidate or party that seems most to coincide with our views. This is not always an easy choice to make. The voter is all too often confused by the multiplicity of issues and pledges. When the candidate gets in, he may carry out the pledges we don't like and forget about those we like.

How often are the voters asked to express their opinion on specific issues, save in Gallup Polls, which are both unofficial and subject to possible error? How often are the really big, important issues put on the line for us to vote yes or no on?

The idea seems to be that the people are not to be trusted, that the politicians and the bureaucrats must make up their minds for them. Yet on the minor and infrequent issues that are put up squarely to the people, it is extraordinary how well the people respond. The New York State Legislature, reflecting the views of certain special interests, says no to a proposal to legalize off-track betting for the benefit of New York City's exchequer. But when the question is put to the people of New York City, they vote better than three to one in favor. Their common sense tells them that this is as harmless and painless a way of raising money for the city treasury as can be devised, all puritanical arguments to the contrary notwithstanding. The people of New Jersey turn down a proposal to issue bonds because their common sense tells them that a bond issue only staves off the evil day when new direct or indirect taxes will have to be imposed, and will make those taxes higher in the long run than a pay-as-you-go policy; it is further quite possible that the same common sense tells them that some of the expenditures contemplated and to be covered by the bond issue are unnecessary. In many local elections, the voters turn down proposals for water fluoridation, or bigger expenditures on specific projects, such as palatial school buildings which are no substitute for real teaching and real learning. It is remarkable what democracy can do if it is only given a chance instead of being treated as a political football.

One wonders what the referendum system on specific issues might be able to accomplish for us on the national scale, even if its results are not made binding upon the legislative, executive and judicial branches of the government. What would a national referendum tell us, for example, about such issues as civil rights or Medicare, farm price supports or right-to-work laws, government subsidies for nonpublic schools or prayer in the classroom? Without going into specific questions of national defense, which are a bit technical these days, it would be interesting to find out how the people feel about non-military foreign aid or our United Nations policy. On a statewide basis, what might a referendum show us concerning requirements for relief and welfare payments, or state-administered unemployment insurance? Again it may be stressed that such referendums need not be binding, but be allowed merely to serve as guides to the politicians and bureaucrats, just in case they really want to know how all the people, rather than a pressure group, feel about a big issue.

This reform, if so it may be styled, goes hand in hand with another. The Constitution provides for occasional constitutional conventions for purposes of amendment. It does not specify that such conventions are to be held at given times, nor does it prescribe the form they are to take. As a result, our Amendments have been added piecemeal, as the occasion for them arose. Some are confusing, if not contradictory. Might they not be clarified by a convention, even if the latter were held only for purposes of airing of issues, discussion and nose-counting?

We occasionally get tired of hearing that "the people" are in favor of certain measures, when there is no direct evidence of the fact, and the measures in question are definitely favored only by legislators and executives who were elected on different issues, and by Justices who were not elected at all.

A convention might propose that the executive and judicial branches of government be shorn of some of the powers and activities that some people say they have wrongly arrogated to themselves. It is equally possible that a convention might wish to add to those powers and legalize them beyond a shadow of a doubt. To cite a few instances:

The Federal Government might conceivably be given either exclusive or concurrent power over education through a constitutional amendment. This may not be so horrible as it sounds to many advocates of states' rights. In most Western democracies, education is a function of the central government, and no unspeakably evil results have occurred in consequence. At any rate, I, for one, would rather see responsibility for the conduct and support of public education placed squarely on the shoulders of the Federal Government than to see it insidiously infiltrate the state educational systems through its system of federal grants accompanied by devious federal controls, which it is in the process of doing now.

The Federal Government assumes a large measure of control over transportation and public carriers. It overrides local laws in the matter of discrimination. Perhaps, in these days of transportation that is overwhelmingly interstate, it ought to assume full control, and override the local laws that prescribe that we shall not have a drink while we are passing through some states whose soil we do not even touch, or be subject to their sales taxes for dining-car meals. A unified railroad system for the country would be an undoubted blessing. The Federal Government may not wish to own and operate the railroads, as many of our sister democracies do with no visible harm to themselves or their democratic institutions; but it could allow and even order the railroads to merge into a single unified network, avoiding the administrative waste and duplication of services of a hundred different and independent railroad lines. It might then be authorized to repeat the operation for air lines, bus lines and shipping.

Modern times demand uniform divorce laws that will have national application and recognition. A giant step in this direction was taken when the states were forced to recognize and respect each other's court decisions in this matter; before that, a person legally divorced and remarried in one state could be guilty of bigamy in another. But the problem goes much deeper. Our divorce laws, where they exist, are hopelessly antiquated. We should have the moral courage either to brand divorce as immoral and ban it altogether, as Italy does, or to recognize it as a social phenomenon that has its *raison d'être* and treat it as such. If we follow the latter course, we should by all means terminate the medieval sham that one of the parties has to be proclaimed guilty of something or other of a heinous nature, and that the divorce is then "awarded" to the other, "aggrieved" party. This procedure lends itself to hypocrisy and lies that are far more immoral than the act of divorce itself, ranging all the way from staged adultery with the active or passive participation of bogus call girls to the vague and often unsubstantiated charge of "mental cruelty" with hired witnesses. If we are going to countenance the institution of divorce, its most favored and least hampered beneficiaries should be two people who have peaceably and honorably agreed to disagree and part company, and who have made mutually satisfactory private arrangements concerning their children and property. In these cases, which might well turn out to be the majority, there should not even be need of lawyers. The court should examine the joint plea to make sure that the arrangement contemplated does not involve injury or injustice to either spouse, their children or anyone else, and simply ratify it, with authorization to both parties to remarry immediately. Even where real litigation is involved, the laws governing divorce should be uniform throughout the nation, and preferably handled by federal courts, in view of the fact that people nowadays move about from state to state far more than they once did, and that the courts of two different states do not always see eye to eye in the matter of alimony and custody and support of children.

There is urgent need of a universal direct primary law by constitutional amendment, to take presidential nominations out of the hands of political bosses in smoke-filled or air-conditioned rooms and put them in the hands of the registered voters of the various parties, where they properly belong. At present, the direct primary, in the few states where it exists, functions very much like a Gallup Poll. It gives some indication of popular preference, but not enough. In the nominating convention of 1952, if the few direct primaries meant anything, the nominees should have been Taft and Kefauver, not Eisenhower and Stevenson. Bossism prevailed. What popular mandate did Dewey have to throw the entire New York delegation, or Warren the entire California delegation, to Eisenhower? And why should Kefauver, who ran and won in every available Democratic primary, have been ditched in favor of a man who did not even bother to seek the support of his party's voters?

Perhaps it is time, in the interests of modern efficiency and economy, to take another look at the antitrust laws, and either repeal them, with some measure of federal control over the highly efficient and economic cartels that might result, or extend them to cover labor unions, which at present constitute by far our biggest, most uncontrolled and most uncontrollable monopolies.

A commission might be set up to investigate and study the need and justification for various federal activities that have grown a hundredfold in the last thirty years, and recommend which among them could safely be discontinued or curtailed, not necessarily all at once, but gradually, over a ten-year period, to give everybody concerned time to adjust. This treatment might well be extended to the farm price support program, which has thrown our entire economy out of kilter and made us noncompetitive on world markets by artificially raising food prices, basic to the cost of living and the cost of doing business, since everyone has to eat. It is quite possible that such a commission, if it were listened to (which the Hoover Commission was not), might cut our spending by 25 to 50 percent, and at the same time double our government's efficiency.

The same commission might well study the unsatisfactory functioning of activities the Federal Government should be responsible for, such as the Post Office. It is ridiculous that in this day and age the inhabitants of the leading nation in the world should be restricted to a single mail delivery a day, with none on Sundays or holidays no one observes, like Veterans' Day, because of the superstitious tradition that the Post Office must be self-supporting. Why must the postal service, one of the few real services the government renders to the individual, be self-supporting when everything else, at home and abroad, is subsidized by the taxpayer?

Democracy, as we said before, is a fine theory. It might even prove successful as a method of government if it were given a real try.

Angry Old Men

WE HAVE LATELY HEARD A GREAT DEAL ABOUT ANGRY young men, who think lots is wrong with the world. Some people attribute their anger to their youth.

Perhaps it isn't quite that simple. Set it down to bad temper, advancing age, or what have you, but there are plenty of men in their advancing years who are also questioning and dissatisfied.

Nor are all of the angry young men of the ultraliberal or Socialistic persuasion. Not too long ago, there was a hassle over the behavior of right-wing Young Republicans in California. They were angry, but not quite in the fashion and for the reasons advocated by our left-wing writers.

I cannot presume to speak for them, but perhaps I can voice the thoughts of the elder group. Some of us are not so terribly old. At any rate, we are not decrepit. Our life expectancy may not be as high as that of the Roosevelt-born generation, but there are yet a few years left. We don't like the setup under which we have to spend them.

You see, we have known a different world, one that antedated the Second World War and the Great Depression. Some of us even remember the world that was before World War One and the New Freedom of the Roaring Twenties.

It had its advantages and its disadvantages. There were not so many material things that people had to have, or so much money to buy them with. But there were compensations. Chief among them was freedom.

Freedom, remember, is a highly relative concept. I know a colleague's Siberian-born wife who served in the Soviet Army during the war, was captured by the Germans, put to work in a labor camp, and finally liberated by the Americans, among whom was her husband-to-be. She claims she was struck by the relative freedom of the Nazi labor camp, as compared with the Soviet Army. The American system that followed the liberation at first impressed her as anarchy. Later she got used to it, and liked it.

But the most striking statement she makes is that when she was a little girl in Siberia, her father would reminisce with her about the good old days of the czars, when there was "freedom" in the Russian land. He spoke of those days with nostalgia, though he led a better material life under the Soviets.

Then there is the story about the old Negro slave who was liberated after the Civil War. A northern newspaperman, sent down South to do a story about the newly liberated Negroes, asked him some pointed questions: "Weren't you better off under your old master? You say he fed you, clothed you, sheltered you, put you to work, and was generally kind to you. Wouldn't you like to be a slave again?" But the old Negro, though tattered and starved, shook his head. "No, suh! Ah likes this loose feelin'!"

Liberty is like that. A paternalistic government, or a Communist one, may be kind, helpful, better for us in a material sense than the loose feeling of being allowed to shift for ourselves and achieve success or failure through our own initiative. But most of us of the older generation, and a good many of the younger, prefer that loose feeling.

The nostalgic feeling of the older ones among us does not consist exclusively of homesickness for the horse and buggy, gaslight and the five-cent cigar or loaf of bread coupled with a one-dollar-a-day wage. We realize that in many respects the world of 1968 is better off than that of 1914. What we hanker for, when you come right down to it, is a combination of the worthwhile features of both. Is there anything really wrong with that? Does our acceptance of the beneficial features of modern progress, coupled with a healthy conservatism for what regards points of view and institutions, make us old mossbacks?

We see no good intrinsic reason why we, and our juniors with us, can't have both liberty *and* prosperity, both TV sets and automobiles *and* freedom from bureaucratic snooping and excessive government control.

It is not eating our cake and wanting it. We are convinced that it is possible to reconcile both things—in fact, that more of our good old-fashioned American freedom from government would lead to far greater material prosperity than we enjoy at present.

But if one or the other must be temporarily sacrificed to achieve a balance (and we are convinced that the sacrifice would be only temporary and partial), then we would rather sacrifice prosperity than liberty. For prosperity is easy to regain, liberty is not; prosperity is contingent, liberty is basic; prosperity is material and matter dies with our bodies, but liberty is of the spirit, and the spirit lives on forever.

Yes, many of us are angry men, angry old men, angry young men, angry middle-aged men. We are angry at bureaucratic stupidity coupled with bureaucratic arrogance, angry at the know-it-all attitude of cocksure experts who want to do things to us "for our own good," angry at the hypocrisy of office-seekers who barter principles for votes.

Above all, we are angry at those who would deprive us of our basic freedoms, hem us in with rules and regulations and restrictions and controls, do things without our knowledge or our consent and then face us with the accomplished fact and a "Too bad! Can't do anything about it any more!" attitude.

They call us conservatives for want of a better name, and because we don't want things and institutions thrown away until we are sure there is a suitable replacement that is also a real improvement. Actually, we are the real progressives, because we believe in orderly, not anarchistic progress; we are the real liberals, because we believe in the liberty of the individual to run his own life, not the liberty of government to run it for him. We are nationalists, because we don't like most of what we see abroad in the way of political institutions. With all our deficiencies, and even now that we are perhaps on the downgrade, our country is still freer and better run than at least 90 per-cent of the rest of the world. The day may be coming, but we still don't have to put up with the equivalent of a Hit-ler or a Stalin, a Castro or a Nasser, a Sukarno or Ben Bella or Tito or Nkrumah. And we propose to keep it that way, if it is at all humanly possible.

Can we? Are there enough of us angry men to halt the headlong rush toward the welfare state? Or do those who are willing to sell their American birthright of freedom for a mess of governmental pottage already outnumber and outvote us?

Liberty has lost enough by default, indifference and compromise, both here and abroad. Somewhere, some-time, there has to be a showdown. We don't propose to have recourse to violence, because we are firm believers in the democratic process and the will of the majority. After all, if the new generations want statism or Commu-nism, they can and should have it, for the future belongs to them, not to us.

But we can endeavor to convince them, by every means in our power, that the Freedom Road to well-being and human happiness is superior to the State-Con-trolled Highway. If they choose not to listen to us, so much the worse for them, far more than for us, whose cycle is nearing completion.

At all events, if we go down, we'll go down fighting.

II
Communism

Communism—And You

THE COMMUNIST BLUEPRINT IS FOR YOU. IT IS NOT JUST for remote lands like Russia and China. It is for the entire world. This means you must study it to see how it will affect you personally, in your private life as an individual, if it succeeds.

In all the countries where the Communists have taken over, from backward, medieval Mongolia to modern, western Czechoslovakia, the same unchanging pattern has been set up. That pattern is no secret. A thousand Iron Curtains cannot hide it. In fact, the Communists are rather proud of it. In a Communist-ruled America, that pattern would be the same.

Your immediate rulers would not be Russians, though Russians might well rule by remote control. They would be Americans, of the type who have been tried and found guilty of plotting to overthrow our present system and of giving our military secrets to our enemies. They would not be elected by you or anyone else, though you might be called on at stated intervals to approve (but not to disapprove) of their rule. They would appoint your legislators, your judges, your government officials, your bureaucrats, your police, even your building superintendent. You would have nothing to say—or if you said it, it would be at your own peril.

The right of opposition and criticism you now enjoy and exercise would be utterly gone. No matter what your

Originally published in *Think,* this piece was reprinted in numerous newspapers and periodicals, including the *Philadelphia Inquirer* and *Catholic Digest,* as well as in the foreign-language editions of *Catholic Digest.*

station in life, you might at first forget yourself and speak out as you do now. You might openly criticize the government or one of its agencies. You might write a letter to the newspapers. That is where you personally would be cracked down upon, until you had learned to hold your tongue and let your thoughts go unspoken and unwritten.

Economically, you would be guaranteed a job, whether you wanted it or not. You would never again run the risk of being unemployed. But you would have little or nothing to say about the nature of your job, its location, or the remuneration you would receive. You would be like a soldier in the army—but your term would never expire.

As a manual worker, you would have no control over wages, hours or working conditions. A strike would be an act of treason against the nation. Your union would be a company union, designed to further the interests of your employer, not your own. The government would be the sole employer. You could change your job or your plant only by special permission.

Your free time would no longer be your own. You might be required to work overtime not for double time, or time and a half, but for nothing. In your leisure hours, you would be expected to join in activities that would be prescribed for you.

As a farmer, at first you would be told exactly what to raise and what not to raise, how much of your product to turn over to the government, how much you could keep for your own use or sell on the open market. But as time went on, the chances are you would be asked to merge your farm with other farms, which you and your fellow-farmers would all cultivate together for the government. In return for this, the government would pay you fixed wages, just as though you worked in a factory.

As an office worker, your salary, hours and terms of employment would be fixed. No change without permission, no employer but the government. As a doctor, lawyer, teacher, professor, nurse, research worker, the same would hold true. As an intellectual, you would have freedom of inquiry and academic freedom only within the bounds prescribed by the government. If your scientific findings, or your artistic or literary output, did not coincide with the Marxist philosophy, you would have to scrap the findings or the output.

In a Communist America, your right to own property would be severely limited. You could own personal things, books, some domestic appliances, articles of clothing, but not productive or semiproductive property, such as a mine, a factory, a large farm, a bank, a store, or even a house or car. If you had a little money, you could invest it in government bonds, but not in stocks or bonds of a private corporation, because there would be none. Insurance would be provided, but only by the government and on the government's terms. Your control over your bank account would be entirely subject to the government's fiscal policy; you might find your dollars reduced overnight to one-tenth their value.

If you belonged to a social class or religious or ethnic group that the government had reason to suspect, you would find yourself, personally, an object of suspicion and treated more harshly than the rest of the population. As a former businessman, for instance, you might be put to hard manual labor, just to prove to you that businessmen were no longer in favor.

Your control over your children would practically cease. The state would prescribe their education and upbringing, and they would be taught to regard family ties as secondary to the ties that bind them to the state and its institutions. Economic pressure would probably force your wife into a job, whether her inclinations ran that way or not.

If you were a member of a religious group, you would probably be allowed to continue in your beliefs. But your right to public worship would be sharply curtailed. Your church would be made an object of ridicule, and its ministers would be harshly dealt with if they dared to open their mouths in reply.

If you were a member of a so-called minority group, you might be granted equality and freedom from discrimination, but only so long as you did not join with your fellow-members of that group in an attempt to preserve your own customs and traditions. Any attempt to resist absorption by the general community, to retain any form of individuality, would lead to deportation and scattering. The equality you would receive would be the equality of slaves, all toiling for the same master.

Who would that master be? In theory, the state. But the state is impersonal. In reality, there would be a new master class of convinced or insincere first-hour Communists, who would be the first to get on the bandwagon. They would get the best jobs, the best housing, the finest cars and food and clothing and amusements and education. They would constitute a new nobility, in all respects similar to the aristocracies of medieval times. You would be the modern serfs.

It isn't likely to happen here, but don't say it *can't* happen. Don't rely on the fact that there are said to be "only" 25,000 or 50,000 or 100,000 Communists in this country. Tiny minorities have seized control of vast countries all through the world's history, by infiltrating key posts, by seizing the sources of material power, by confusing and cowing big, unorganized majorities.

If you don't like the picture we have painted (and we have by no means painted it in the most lurid colors), be on your guard. Liberty is easy to lose, hard to regain.

The Question No Communist Can Answer

AMONG THE MORE DISQUIETING SIGNS OF THE PRESENT age is the race, on the part of human beings born free, to become slaves.

In France, one-fourth of the population votes the Com-

Originally published in *Saturday Evening Post*. Reprinted in *Reader's Digest* under the title "The Basic Freedom," and in all the international editions of *Reader's Digest*.

munist ticket. In Italy, it is one-third. The nations of western Europe, the Near East, southeastern Asia, Africa, have to be bribed to remain free.

Ah, but is it freedom? ask the Communist propagandists. Real freedom is economic security, racial equality, "human rights." The UN, with its Human Rights Commission, aids and abets this propaganda. Misguided idealists in Britain and America follow this line, and raise doubts as to whether ours or the Soviets' is the true concept of freedom.

There is a simple way of finding out. Ask the people behind the Iron Curtain, the men and women who risk their lives to get out to where freedom is. Ask the Poles who steal their nation's army planes, the Czechs who forge military tanks, the Hungarians who break across fields of barbed wire, the East Germans who lose their lives in vain attempts to get over the Berlin Wall. Ask the North Korean and Chinese prisoners who don't want to go home to Communism, and whom the Communists insist on bringing back home at all costs. They will tell you where freedom is, and who has it.

But more than that, they will give you a definition and test of freedom so simple that it takes no scholars or philosophers to grasp it.

Freedom is where you can get out if you want to. Freedom is where if you don't like it you are at liberty to go away. That is your key test—the right to quit.

In America, Britain, and the nations of the West generally, we take this right for granted. Anyone who doesn't like the existing setup is free to get out. This goes for the individual and the group. It goes for the worker who doesn't like his job. It goes for the person who doesn't care for his surroundings. It goes for the person who is a victim of racial or religious discrimination in some sections, but finds that he can move away to other sections, where there is no discrimination. It goes even for the Communist sympathizer who wants to go off to the Communist paradise.

Behind the Iron Curtain this basic freedom is wanting. If you don't like the way things are run in Poland, Czechoslovakia, Hungary or Russia, you nevertheless have to stay there. If you try to go, you take your life in your hands. If you want to break away from your job, your home, your nation, you have to get permission—or else.

That is the basic difference between our way of life and theirs—the right to quit, the right to emigrate, the right to get out. If anyone cares to think about it, he will quickly perceive that here is the basic human right, the basic freedom, outweighing by far all the mealy-mouthed "human rights" that are prated of in UN councils.

The freedom to get out is what distinguishes a free man from a slave. What was the slavery of ancient times, or the slavery of the American plantations, but the denial of the right to go one's way if one didn't like it? Many of the ancient and recent slaves had good food, good treatment, lifelong security. But they couldn't go away.

This should be pondered well by the Communist voters of western Europe, of Latin America, of Southeast Asia. It should be pondered well by the doubting Thomases in our own midst, whenever their doubts assail them.

There are worse evils than economic inequality, social prejudice, racial or religious discrimination. Surely these are bad enough, but if the worst comes to the worst, any free individual can remedy these evils for himself, by the simple expedient of moving away from them. The biggest social evil of all is slavery, and slavery is the denial of the right to move away. The abolition of slavery, of serfdom, of the forcible attachment of the individual to the soil, or the job, or the master, was the greatest achievement of modern enlightenment.

Communism, by its principles and practices, brings back human slavery. Between it and truly free men there can be no compromise.

The Threefold Challenge of Communism

WHAT MANY OF US, IN OUR STRUGGLE AGAINST COMMUNISM, have not yet perceived or analyzed is the mighty threefold appeal of Communism to the masses of all countries.

To a world that is tired of depressions, recessions, unemployment and economic insecurity, Communism holds out the lure of a society in which poverty, need and hunger will be banished. To a world grown tired of hatreds and persecutions that have their root in racial discrimination, Communism presents the boon of racial equality. To a world grown weary of war, Communism offers the promise of enduring peace.

Whether these promises are meant to be kept is another matter. The information that reaches us across the Iron Curtain indicates that they are not. But the propaganda continues to be drummed in, here and abroad, by every means that a skillful and highly organized machine can devise.

We can oppose this propaganda by denying its sincerity, as we have been doing. The contest then degenerates into something similar to the "Yes, you are!"—"No, I ain't!" of two children. Meanwhile, a certain number of people (not a majority, but the sort of significant minority that the Communists deem sufficient for their purpose) will be taken in by Communist claims.

We can also expose the fundamental mendacity of Communist propaganda in claiming that Communism is the originator and standard-bearer of the three great and essentially desirable reforms it purports to advocate—

economic security for the masses, the brotherhood of man, and a warless world.

As a matter of fact, Communists are shameless plagiarists. The three great features of their system were devised not by them, but by the Christian Church. They are Christianity's inventions, not Marxism's. If the Christian world has not yet brought them to completion and fulfillment, neither has the Marxist. But the Christian world devised them. Communism has only stolen them.

Granting that economic security for all could exist in an ideal Communist society, which so far has not materialized, it could with equal and greater ease exist in an ideal Christian society, which, however imperfect it may have been in past centuries, has at least proved itself.

Economic *equality,* that tenet of Marxism whereby all share equally in society's productivity, regardless of their individual contributions to it, has, of course, been scrapped long ago by the Marxists themselves, who found it impractical. Today, in Communist countries, there are vast discrepancies in individual income and living standards. The sort of economic equality that Marxist theorists envisaged has been successful, as a matter of fact, only in Christian monastic orders.

We are left, then, with economic *security* as the sole surviving economic goal of Communism. Such economic security came far closer to realization in the Christian Middle Ages than it did before, under individualistic paganism, or has since, under the "enlightened" bourgeois capitalism of the eighteenth and nineteenth centuries or the "scientific" Sovietism of today.

In the Middle Ages, when the Church was supreme, there was economic security, within the limitations of a mechanically backward civilization, for all social classes —the royalty and nobility whose mission it was to defend Christendom; the clergy, upon whom devolved the task of ministering to the spiritual needs of the population; the artisans, whose Christian guilds antedate by centuries the achievements of modern labor unions; the peasants, protected from oppression by the laws of the Church; and even the penniless, whom the churches fed and sheltered in accordance with a system not unlike that of the modern relief rolls. The Church, that great custodian and depository of medieval wealth, acted as a steward, receiving from the rich and dispensing to the poor; it acted as a labor moderator, mediator and arbiter; it reconciled the interests of the various social classes; it constantly reminded all, rich and poor, noble and lowborn, that there is no essential difference among human beings, that all are endowed with an immortal soul and equal in the eyes of God. Kings, nobles and prelates enjoyed a larger share of the total available wealth than did peasants, artisans and beggars, just as commissars, scientists and Stakhanovite workers in the Soviet Union today enjoy a higher standard of living than the mass of the population. But the lower classes were never without the protection and material aid of their church. Economic security, within the bounds of the attainable, was attained in the Christian Middle Ages.

Racial equality and the brotherhood of man are advanced by the modern Communists as their own special discovery. They claim a monopoly on the idea. Christians should rise to point out that long before Marx, Engels, Lenin or Stalin, the brotherhood of man was preached by the Church of Christ. It was perhaps this equalitarian ideal that contributed most to the overwhelming triumph of Christianity in its early centuries. Mankind was ripe then, as it is now, for the overthrow of the pagan principle of inherently superior and inferior human beings. Centuries before Lincoln proclaimed that all men are created equal, this pronouncement had appeared in the teachings of Christ and the writings of the Church Fathers. As for racial discrimination, not even the Church's worst enemies have been able to point to instances of it in the Church's early history. Slaves and masters became equal in the secret rites of the catacombs. As Christianity spread, the most varied races and colors came under its sheltering wings. No race, however backward, was ever deemed unworthy of conversion and redemption by Christian missionaries. Black, yellow, red and brown bishops, priests and ministers have been and are ordained. In Catholic countries especially, there is no color line, no racial prejudice. The Christian Middle Ages, with Latin as their universal tongue, with their universities that admitted all qualified comers, of whatever race or nationality, with their ecclesiastical organization that knew no national boundaries, have come closer to the goal of racial equality and universality, of the brotherhood of man under the fatherhood of God, than the "enlightened" centuries of liberalism, that saw the establishment of national churches, the rise of rampant nationalisms, and the growth of racial ideologies that would have seemed highly grotesque to those living in the so-called Dark Ages.

War as a means of settling disputes is as old as mankind. In a society based on the rule of force, Christ's command to Peter to put up his sword came with the force of a mighty clarion call. The early Church condemned war for any and all purposes, even in self-defense. It has been charged that this pacifistic attitude of the Christian Church led to the downfall of the Roman Empire and the triumph of the barbarian invasions. It is more likely that the Roman Empire, having lived by the sword, was doomed to perish by the sword. The Church of Christ, on the other hand, not only survived, but triumphed over all the bloodthirsty invaders that came into contact with it, winning them over to itself by its tenets of peace. What, in all human history, is more miraculous, more unheard-of, than that fierce, war-loving tribes like the Goths and the Franks, the Vandals and the Longobards, the Anglo-Saxons and the Danes should succumb to the Word of the Prince of Peace, and join His flock? If any historical proof were needed of the divine origin of Christ's Church, this would indeed be proof.

Barbarian customs and blood-lusts could not be turned overnight into lamblike habits. Converted pagans continued to bare their swords. Throughout the Middle Ages, however, the Church continued to exercise its office as a moderator of fierce reversals to type. The Law of Sanctuary, the Truce of God, the innumerable occasions on which the Church intervened to put an end to fratricidal strife, are there to show that insofar as peace could be advocated and achieved in those troublous times, the Christian Church advocated and achieved it.

Christians today face what will perhaps be the greatest menace to their church and their faith. Communism is a relentless, fanatical, insidious foe. Where it can seize power openly and crush its opponents by main force, it does so. Where it cannot, it infiltrates. It sings a siren song of social and economic equality, of racial brotherhood, of universal peace to the world's weary and unwary masses. Therein lies its appeal and its greatest danger. If the Communists everywhere behaved as they have in Poland, Yugoslavia, Hungary, Russia, China, Cuba, Korea, Tibet and Vietnam, they would be less of a menace. But in the Western World they put on sheep's clothing and offer their triple program of bread, brotherhood and peace, as though it were something new and never before heard of.

It is upon this arrogation of the invention of three highly desirable things that Christians must center their attacks. Communism must not be allowed to capitalize on the desire of the masses for three worthy objectives, presented by the Communists as their own monopoly. Christians must present their prior claim to the ideas, and their record of success in attaining them.

"Better Red Than Dead"

I SAW THESE WORDS IN A TV NEWSCAST. THEY WERE inscribed in large letters on a poster carried by a young woman who also wheeled a baby carriage, on a picket line of demonstrators against President Kennedy's somewhat belated action in the Cuban crisis.

Who were you, little lady with the poster and the baby carriage? You and your child looked healthy, well-fed, well-clad, typical middle-class Americans. You were pretty. You looked as though you might have been brought up on good Florida orange juice and Wisconsin unskimmed milk, poured into you unstintingly by a free American economy, not doled out with a dropper by a Red bureaucrat.

Did that poster really voice your sentiments? Did you really mean that you'd rather see that chubby baby of yours raised under the shadow of Red gangsterism, brought up as a little slave to Big Brother, deprived of his freedom of choice and the right to think for himself, living out his life under the Red terror, than to see him quickly, painlessly obliterated in a blinding flash, along with you, me, and the rest of us Americans, if it really came to a showdown?

Remember, little lady, we do not avoid death by postponing it. Eventually we must all go; if not by the hydrogen bomb, then by lung cancer, from smoking too many good cigarettes and inhaling too many automobile fumes; if not by a rifle bullet, then by Bright's disease, brought about by drinking too much good bourbon; if not by a bayonet, then by a coronary, due to too much cholesterol in our rich American diet. Or perhaps just by a stray virus, which can hit anybody.

So what you're buying by submitting to the world's Castros and Maos and Khrushchevs is not life, but time. Time to do what? Time to live how? Quaking every minute? Fearing for your own life and that of your loved ones? Bowing and submitting and paying lip service to all sorts of principles that your heart and your brain reject as utterly false, utterly harmful?

Does it mean nothing to you that thousands of people like yourself, in Cuba, at the Berlin Wall, in Hungary, in Red China, have preferred to part with life rather than submit to being dehumanized and turned into robots of the all-powerful Red State? They, too, may at one time have said: "Better Red than dead." But later on, they found they couldn't take it. So their motto changed to an earlier one, one that happens to be American, but appeals to free men and women everywhere: "Give me liberty or give me death." And, the way the cards were stacked, many of them got death.

Life is not the greatest boon, little lady with the baby carriage. Because life, no matter how you stretch it, is not eternal. But other things are: honor, conscience, self-respect; above all, freedom. The freedom to choose for yourself, to be yourself, even to be dead a few years sooner, if necessary.

Ten, twenty, a hundred, a thousand years from now, we shall all be dead, equally dead. But there will be a difference in how we died. With our heads high, fearlessly facing those who would enslave us, or as abject, crawling creatures, afraid to look up into the faces of the world's tyrants and butchers of men? We have a choice, you see, as to whether this universal death that reaches out to all of us without exception will find us standing or crouching, an object of admiration or of scorn, partly to those who come after us, but most of all to ourselves.

Think it over, pretty little lady with the poster and the chubby baby.

Little Chats With A Marxist

We Don't *Want to Bury You*

"The Soviet Dream is of a society where all men will be proletarians. The American Dream is of a society where all men will be property owners."

OF COURSE YOU DIDN'T MEAN IT LITERALLY, MR. KHRUSHCHEV, when you said you would bury us. What you meant was that your system would bury ours.

We have news for you. We don't want to bury you, either literally or figuratively. All we want to do to you and the Russian people is to help set you free, resurrect you, bring you back to life. Because you, too, are human. Within your breasts there beats the same heart of man that pounds within us, telling us, with each beat, seventy-two times a minute, that we are born to be free, free,

free! We want to see you throw off your ideological chains, so that we may embrace you as our brothers.

We know the stuff you are made of. We have seen you Russians fighting in the name of home and freedom against the forces of tyranny, breaking the iron circle of your would-be enslavers at Stalingrad, pressing back the powers of darkness as time and again in your history you pressed back those who wanted to destroy your independence, from the Tatars and Mongols to the armies of Napoleon. We have thrilled to the music of your composers, the beauty of your dances, the achievements of your poets and writers and scientists. We respect you and admire you for what you really are, not for what you profess to be. We want you free, by our side, so that we may march on together to greater achievement in the name of our common humanity. No, we emphatically do not want to bury you!

Right now we mourn for you. But we know you will rise again. Communism is a passing phase, but the Russian people are eternal. You will be standing beside us long after the baneful shadows of Marx and Engels and Lenin and Stalin have passed from the face of the earth.

You say we are aggressors, imperialists. Sometimes your generals, in their saber-rattling speeches made for home consumption, claim we want to destroy you. Stop and think a moment. If we had been so minded, we could have done it with relative ease back in 1945, right after the fall of Nazi Germany. You were exhausted, bled white by your mighty war effort; we were comparatively fresh. Your manhood had been depleted by the tremendous losses you had suffered retreating before the Nazi hordes, then driving them back to their own border and beyond. We, too, had suffered losses, but nowhere like your own. Our armies were intact, fully equipped, ready to march. Above all, we had the atom bomb that had brought Japan to her knees, along with the mightiest air force the world has ever known, prepared to deliver it to all your cities, production centers and strongholds. You had nothing to retaliate with. Had we been the aggressors and imperialists you describe us to be, it would have been so easy to pick a quarrel with you and overwhelm you, as Bulgaria's allies overwhelmed the country that in the Balkan War of 1912 had brought down the Turkish Empire almost single-handed.

At the very least, we could have seized Berlin, all of East Germany, Austria, Czechoslovakia, Hungary, the Balkans, and left you with the shreds of a common victory. Does it mean nothing to you that instead we chose to honor, and more than honor, all the commitments we had made, perhaps foolishly, when you were engaged in a life-and-death struggle and we were waiting for the proper moment to pounce upon the common enemy?

It is quite possible that the historians of the future will sharply criticize us for our idealism and honesty in not seizing world dominion when we had the chance, in allowing you to share with us the fruits of victory and world power when we could so easily have shut you out. But if there is a shred of honesty in those same future historians, they will never charge us with aggressive, imperialistic aims or ambitions. Fools we may have been; ruthless, selfish grabbers of land and power, never.

We offered you, too, Marshall Plan aid for the reconstruction of your war-torn country, the same sort of aid that set western Europe back on its feet. You, in your justifiable but excessive pride, turned down our offer. You chose to rebuild your land with your own resources. For that we honor and admire you, even while we regret your choice, for acceptance would have bound us in indissoluble friendship.

We really believe in peaceful coexistence. We do not view it as a device whereby to prepare for new wars, or to weaken the will and internal structure of the country with which we coexist until such a time as we can overthrow it by force. We have proved it not only in the case of those Asian and African nations which we have helped to independence and nationhood, not only with nations whose political structure and economic system resemble our own, but even with your fellow-Communist countries, Yugoslavia and Poland. Strange as it may strike you, we want other nations to have the system of government they themselves favor. All we want to make sure of is that it isn't the system someone else picks for them. This is one of the main sources of disagreement between us.

As far as the systems themselves are concerned, we shall discuss them later. There is one basic principle, however, where our ideal differs from yours. You dream of a classless society where every man will be a proletarian, all other social classes having disappeared, by violence or otherwise. We Americans, too, have a dream. It is not so drastic as yours, nor does it call for a fixed timetable. But it is just as equalitarian as yours, in its own way. The American dream is of a society in which all men, to a greater or lesser degree, will be property owners (call them capitalists or members of the bourgeoisie if you like). We want each and every member of our society to have a personal stake, a personal interest, in our productive machinery, not the sort of impersonal, problematical interest that is supposed to arise but fails to, because human nature makes no provision for it, when the state owns and runs everything, and every man works for the state as he would for a private employer.

We have further news for you. We are well on the way to realizing our dream. Stockholders, bondholders, holders of insurance policies and bank accounts, home owners, property owners of all kinds now constitute at least two-thirds of our population, and we are confidently looking forward to the day when all men and women in our capitalistic society will be property owners. Our people like it that way. Your people would, too, if they had a chance at it.

The "Inevitability" of Communism

"The Millennium is as old as the hills."

IT HAS TO HAPPEN, YOU SAY. AS TIME GOES ON, THE COMmunist system will prove so superior to capitalism in giving the people everything they want that the masses in the capitalistic countries will clamor for it and fight for it. At this point, the capitalistic countries, worn out by their international, colonial and internal conflicts, will fall into your lap like ripe pears from a tree, and all the world will be one.

Of course, all this hasn't happened yet. If you really expected the theory to work, you could afford to sit back, cultivate your own economy, usher in the millennium in the countries you control, and comfortably wait for the good example to be followed everywhere. This emphatically you do not do. Everywhere you agitate, plot, organize for violent action. In many lands, notably China, Korea, Vietnam, Laos, Cuba, you have had to resort to armed aggression to bring about what you claim is inevitable. In these cases, the decision has rested not with the people concerned, not with principles or precepts, but with force of arms. Force of arms proves who is stronger, not who is right. Above all, force of arms does not prove the inevitability of anything, save force of arms itself.

On the purely ideological plane, you make your appeal to the masses by promising them a better material life. How well have you kept that promise? Is the population of East Germany better off materially than that of West Germany? If so, why do so many East Germans want to get away to West Germany that you have had to erect the Berlin Wall and shoot down anyone who wants to defect? Are North Korea and North Vietnam better off economically than South Korea and South Vietnam? Is the Chinese mainland more prosperous than Formosa? Why do so many Chinese pile out of Red China into Hong Kong and Macao? Why do so many Cubans pile into Miami? Can you really convince anyone of the superiority of your system, not on ideological grounds, not in connection with personal freedom, but on a purely material, economic basis? Even in your own Soviet Union, where the noble experiment has been going on since 1917, how do living standards compare with, say, old, "decadent" Britain or France, let alone the United States?

The fact of the matter is that the Millennium is as old as the hills. Since the dawn of history, individual parties, groups and movements have been making promises of a material nature. "Join us, follow our movement, and you will lead a far better, more enjoyable life." The promise is seldom kept.

The movements that have permanently succeeded are the ones that promised no material blessings, but rather blood, sweat and tears, like Christianity and Buddhism. At the very most, they are movements that have promised material blessings only as a corollary to something spiritual and metaphysical, like the doctrine of personal liberty and individual freedom, a doctrine that began with England's Magna Charta, continued with the French Revolution and its Rights of Man, and had its full embodiment in the American Declaration of Independence and Constitution. It is of interest that none of these movements promised material blessings, save perhaps as an unspoken consequence. The mainspring of all of them is principle, not matter, the principle of individual freedom, of equality under the law, of human brotherhood.

Your dialectic materialism denies the metaphysical and spiritual. In considering man's material wants as paramount, it degrades man to the level of an animal. But even the animal dislikes being caged. Ideally, a Communist country is a vast gilded cage, supplied with all animal comforts. Actually, it is something less, far less.

There are some who listen to your promises and believe them. But then, there have always been believers in the Millennium—Eldorado, the golden cities of Cibola, the Fountain of Youth. Yours is no new discovery. Those who believe in your Millennium are doomed to disappointment, as were all their precursors.

Communism is far from inevitable. There are other, more practical, less visionary, infinitely less drastic ways of achieving not the Millennium, but a well-ordered, decent, reasonably prosperous society in which all men will share equally of freedom, justice and opportunity—three things that matter far more than material blessings.

The Doctrine of Love and Hate

"What you can't remedy, destroy! What you can't reform, liquidate!"

YOU PROFESS TO LOVE MANKIND. YOUR DOCTRINE, LIKE your *Internationale,* is for the entire human race. Your classless society is meant to embrace all of mankind.

But your practice is in conflict with your theory, unless we assume that while you love mankind in the abstract, you hate selected portions of it to the point of wanting to destroy them physically. The gospel you preach to the proletarian masses is not one of love, like that of Christianity. It is one of bitter, unrelenting hatred.

You want to build. But before you can build, you claim you must destroy. Hence you do not hesitate to go into a community that is basically progressive, satisfied and reasonably happy and prosperous, and sow into its midst the seeds of discord and strife, of hatred and intolerance. This you do on the pretext that you must tear down the existing structure, with its good as well as its bad features, in order to erect a better, indeed, a perfect one.

The history that you profess to study informs you that true social progress in the past has been achieved gradually, not overnight, by basically peaceful means rather than by violence, though doses of the latter have occasionally been necessary. But in this respect you scorn the lessons of history.

You scorn compromise, though you firmly believe in false, hypocritical appeasement and temporary coalitions for the sake of winning your objective. Whoever may have first coined the slogan that "the end justifies the means," you have made it yours, and applied it to the hilt.

You profess to believe that all evils can be corrected

by education and environment, but you are the first to admit that education and environment work slowly. Accordingly, to obtain faster results, you have coined another slogan: "What you can't quickly remedy, destroy! What you can't quickly reform, liquidate!" This you apply to all who oppose you.

You decry intolerance in others, but you are the most intolerant sect the world has ever known. Your dogmatism dwarfs that of any medieval church. Your inquisition puts Torquemada's to shame. You don't shrink from torture, brainwashing, or treating the individual like one of Pavlov's dogs.

But above all, you hate. You hate institutions, regardless of their praiseworthy features. You hate ideologies that differ from your own. You hate happiness and prosperity brought about by any method other than yours. You may, in the long run, want to build up. But for the time being, your motto is "Destroy, destroy, destroy!"

Don't complain if some of your mad-dog tactics are occasionally employed against you. In the face of the Budapest tanks and the shootings at the Berlin Wall, don't shout "Police brutality!" if someone carries you bodily out of a Congressional hearing where you are creating a disturbance. It's the least you can expect. Not even Christians invariably turn the other cheek.

You need to revise not only your ideas, but also your methods. The game of violence is one at which more than one can play.

Love Without God

"We have traveled far into outer space; we have not found God!"

FINE, COMRADE COSMONAUTS, FINE! WHAT YOU SAY DOES not surprise us. But there is one question that puzzles us. Just what *did* you expect to find out in outer space? An old gentleman with a long white beard and flowing garments, sitting majestically on a pink cloud? A swarm of angels, beautiful sexless beings with great white wings and halos, some armed with flaming swords, others strumming on harps?

Come, come, Comrades, don't be so old-fashioned! Don't you know that the anthropomorphic concept of God you have in mind went out of style centuries ago?

But the spiritual concept of God remains, and will always remain. If God did not exist, modern civilized man would have to create Him, because his civilization could not endure otherwise.

You profess to believe in dialectic Marxist materialism. To paraphrase the statement of belief of one of our Christian groups, to you "there is no spirit; all is infinite matter." Have you ever stopped to think of the implications of this belief?

If all is matter, including man, then man is just another animal, endowed with a few billion more nerve connections than his fellow-animals, but an animal nevertheless. This would entitle him to behave like an animal. Animals have few and doubtful social instincts. They are, for the most part, supremely and unashamedly selfish, obeying the material laws of self-preservation, self-gratification and self-reproduction. Where animals live in family groups, there is generally, but not universally, a natural instinct on the part of the mother to protect her young. This instinct is generally not shared by the father, who as often as not will kill or devour his own progeny, and in the mother it endures only so long as the young are helpless. (Don't ask us, by the way, who put it there. If you don't know, we refuse to tell you.) There is no corresponding instinct on the part of the younger generations to protect or feed their elders. Even where animals live and operate in communities, like the bees or the ants, it cannot be proved that the individual is prompted by a true social instinct, set apart from the instinct for self-preservation. The animal is normally a shameless individualist, existing for himself and his own pleasure.

This makes the animal, who embodies the principles of your dialectic materialism, the very opposite of your social ideal. You want men to live in communities, to think along lines of community, not individual welfare, even to sacrifice themselves for the community. But a materialistic view of the universe excludes any kind of loyalty outside of one's own self. Loyalty to the family, to the group, to the nation, are by definition excluded from the true materialistic concept of existence. The latter implies only complete and utter self-seeking and personal advantage.

In the same breath that you decry the old, outworn bourgeois virtues of loyalty to a family, a nation, a faith, you revive these outworn notions for your own purposes. You are justly proud of the heroism of your war heroes. But if the materialistic view is correct, why should anyone behave heroically? Materialistically speaking, the advantage to your individual soldiers in the face of the Nazi invaders should have been to run away and save their own skins, not to stand and risk extinction. Why die in war—any kind of war, bourgeois or proletarian? Yet they stood and died. They were not following the doctrine of Marxist materialism, but rather a form of sublime idealism worthy of an obscurantistic past. Shall we say they died for Stalin, as the Russians of old died for the czar? Or for Mother Russia, now transformed into a Soviet Union? Or for a concept of right and freedom that comes dangerously close to the one by which our capitalistic nations operate, at least in theory?

If one of you (or one of us, for that matter) accepts the doctrine of materialism at full face value, then he is justified in committing all the acts which both you and we consider antisocial. Materialistically speaking, how can you prove that it is wrong for the individual to take what he wants, without consideration or regard for others? The animal, who behaves materialistically, does just that. If he is hungry, he kills in order to eat. If he wants a desirable lair, he will kill or drive out its former occupant. If he wants sexual gratification, he takes over the herd, provided he is strong enough to do it.

If you live by the doctrine of materialism, how can you prove that it is wrong for me to take what belongs to another, to kill another if he stands in my way, to attack and rape any woman who seizes my fancy? Your dialectic materialism offers the biggest justification for the evils of feudalism, or for the one-man, strong-man rule you profess to abhor, but to which you subscribe in practice. Materialism means only the rule of force, the cult of strength. Winner take all. It means kill off the weak and old and infirm, not to everyone according to his needs.

Actually, what you have done is to take the old bourgeois virtues, give them a brushing and a coat of polish, and put them back into circulation. You have now restored the family unit, you have brought back discipline and respect for authority, friendship, love and marriage; you frown on divorce, on hoodlumism, on improper, inconsiderate, even impolite behavior. You have brought back the cult of the fatherland, and you no longer equate it with the world at large.

You have not yet brought back God, but you will. You will, because God is what supplies the mainspring for and gives a reason for existence to all those virtues that we hold in common, and that you have resurrected. Social virtues do not spring from materialism, which is basically antisocial and individualistic to a point far beyond what even we are willing to accept. Social virtues are based squarely upon a spiritual interpretation of the universe, and that means God, by whatever name you choose to call Him. Matter knows no virtues, social or otherwise, because it is inert. Spirit does, because it is alive. Spirit, not matter, inspires the code of behavior that you, along with us, deem desirable.

We have the edge on you, because we have held on to that code all the way through. Don't make the mistake of equating the Judeo-Christian code, which is essentially the code of all believers in God and spirit, with those bourgeois "virtues" that you deplore. What you deplore are the bourgeois vices, and we deplore them with you, for they mark a fall from grace, a deviation from God's code.

Don't take too much comfort, either, from the fact that we have not always lived up to God's code. Only Christ lived up to it in full. All we can do, as fallible human beings, is to try to imitate His example. But if we fall from grace, we do so with the consciousness that we are falling, and with a sense of regret and remorse, coupled with a determination to do better next time.

God is not to be found on a pink cloud in outer space, Comrades, though He undoubtedly permeates that space. He is to be found within the heart of man, including Soviet man.

Communism Is Old-Fashioned

"Plus ça change, plus c'est la même chose."

THERE IS NOT TOO MUCH ABOUT YOU THAT IS FUNNY. FOR the most part, everything connected with you, your philosophy, your principles, your practices and methods, is tragic. But once in a while you succeed in bringing a smile to our lips. This happens especially when you claim to have invented the way of life of the future, to be the standard-bearers of a new civilization, the harbingers of ideas that have never been advanced before.

In reality, everything about your doctrines, your beliefs, even your behavior, is ancient, antiquated, stale. There is not a single novel feature in anything you do or advocate. It has all been presented and done before, to the point where the world has grown heartily sick and tired of it all. If mankind is to have something new and better, it will have to come from us, not from you. Shall we prove it?

You object to rule by one man, to rule by divine right. So far, all you have been able to show is a series of dictators, strong-arm men, gang leaders. A few of them are also demagogues, like Tito and Castro. The majority of them are strong, silent men, like Stalin and Mao, men who don't care whether they are popular among the masses or not, even on a fraudulent basis. You have pushed the political bossism which is one of the banes of our Western democracies to its outermost limits. But more than that, you have brought back autocracy and divine right, though you don't call it that. In Western democracies worthy of the name, we have the right of opposition and some semblance of political parties, along with some measure of choice by the masses that are governed as to who shall govern. This, incidentally, works out to your advantage, because your Communist parties are seldom outlawed, as they should be, and are able to carry out the functions of an opposition party. When have you ever tolerated opposition, organized or not, or free elections where the voters had the right to choose between two or more alternatives? Did your most recent autocrat, Fidel Castro, permit any sort of free election in Cuba when he took over, although he had promised one while Batista was in power? You have put us squarely back into the Middle Ages at their darkest.

You profess to want to get rid of class differences. You decry blood aristocracy. What have you given us but a "New Class," as one of your writers so aptly put it? Your Communist bureaucrats form the new aristocracy, enjoying the best of material existence there is to be enjoyed in the countries you control. There are even disquieting signs that you are in the process of forming a new blood aristocracy, with the people in control passing on their privileges to their descendants. So much for your classless society.

You were going to get rid of nationalism, a purely bourgeois institution. No more antipathies, no more irredentism, no more wars. You began by creating a new Russian nationalism, which proceeded to swallow up nations and parts of nations that did not want to be swallowed: selected portions of Germany, Poland, Finland, Romania, even the tail of Czechoslovakia; all of Lithuania, Estonia, Latvia; and this without even the hypocritical gesture of a plebiscite. Then you developed a new Chinese nationalism, which made itself felt in Mongolia, Manchuria, North Korea, North Vietnam, Tibet, Laos, Cambodia, even Burma and Thailand and Indonesia, where the Chinese are encouraged to remain Chinese and not amalgamate with the native populations. You have been masters at the art of creating and fostering nationalisms and irredentisms even where they did not exist before, as in the Arab and African nations; some of this has backfired, and you have found yourselves hoisted with your own petard, when after having fanned into being a black nationalism you discovered that the Africans dislike you because your skins are white.

"Anticolonialism" is one of your most revered slogans. Some say you have bamboozled the Western nations into giving up their colonial possessions so that you could take them over. At any rate, what better episodes of modern colonialism can be advanced than your stifling of Hungarian and Polish independence, or the Chinese takeover in Tibet, followed by aggression in India? And what of the colonial populations you hold under your Russian thumbs? Do you grant full equality to the yellow-skinned populations on your soil? Why is it that your top councils do not include a single Uzbek, or Tadzhik, or Kazakh, or Turkoman? Who has a better chance to get somewhere in life, a Negro with us or a Mongol with you?

The very basis of your economic philosophy is the public ownership and operation of the means of production. This is trumpeted as a great innovation. When the Romans first came into Gaul, they found the Gaulish tribes living under a system of primitive Communism quite reminiscent of your collective farms. The soil was common property, all participated in tilling it and harvesting the produce, which was then stored in common storehouses and distributed by the headman of the tribe ("From each according to his capability, to each according to his needs"). The Romans, however, were primitive capitalists. They believed in private property, with each man owning and operating his own little plot. This system they taught to the Gauls, who took to it like ducks to water, and have been hanging on to it ever since. Nowhere is the farmer so attached to his own soil and private property as he is in France.

The Chinese Reds tried instituting the segregation of the sexes, with all the men living communally in one big house, all the women and children in another, and the two sexes coming together only at stated times, for breeding purposes. Whatever merit there may be in this system, it is far from new. The ancient Spartans had it.

Forced labor, with every man employed by the state, fed by the state, and compelled to stick to his job, goes all the way back to ancient Egypt, where the Pharaohs used the system to construct their pyramids. The system of mass deportations, which you have practiced so effectively in the case of the Volga Kalmuks, the Sudeten Germans, the Silesians and East and West Prussians, not to mention the upper classes of the Baltic States, was a favorite device of the Romans whenever they were faced with recalcitrant populations. They scattered the Oscans in this fashion after the Social War. The only time they failed was when they tried to destroy the unity of the Jews by scattering them over the North African coast. Those same Jews are defying you today.

Even your basic Communist philosophy, if we put it on the highest and most dignified and idealistic plane and shear away from it its more unpleasant manifestations, appears in practically modern form in Plato's *Republic.* Plato describes an ideal state, such as you envisage, where an intellectual elite runs the show, and lesser intellects obey.

Just what have you contributed to the philosophy of government that hasn't been tried and found wanting in the past? Just where is the originality of your Communist thinkers, your Marxes and Engels and Lenins? You are dishing up for the consumption of the world's masses an ancient stew that has been simmering along since the days of the pyramids and the ziggurats. It is truly an *olla podrida,* and offends sensitive nostrils. It may work with a few backward groups who have never known anything better, or different. But don't try to ram it down the throats of people who have in their background the free Greek and Italian city-states, the medieval guilds, the Magna Charta, the Declaration of the Rights of Man, the Declaration of Independence, and the American Constitution.

III

International Relations

The American Heritage

WHEN I ARRIVED IN AMERICA IN 1908, THERE WERE FEW automobiles and no TV sets. Mechanically and industrially, the country had barely begun to advance beyond the civilized lands of western Europe. But there was one important characteristic that distinguished all Americans, whether native or foreign-born. It was intense pride in their political institutions and economic achievements. They had taken a vast, undeveloped continent and turned it into a major power by the sweat of their brows and the genius of their brains. Further, they had given the world a working model of a state where national power and prestige were reconciled with maximum freedom for the individual. Americans were justifiably and without exception proud to be Americans.

In that horse-and-buggy America there was no trace of the apologetic undertone that has of late become the vogue in certain circles. We, as Americans, did not feel we had to offer excuses for the prosperity we had built with our own hands to people who lived in nations perhaps less fortunate, but perhaps also less energetic and dynamic. We did not feel we had to present apologies for the few minor defects in our social and economic structure, because a great many of us knew, from first-hand experience, that far graver defects existed everywhere else. We seldom, if ever, worried about what country X or country Y would think of our policies, foreign or internal. The country's mood was one of intense, patriotic pride in what it had done and was doing. There may even have been a little touch of defiance in that pride.

Originally published under the title "Why Do So Many Americans Apologize for Their Country?" in *Saturday Evening Post.*

There had been wars in our history, but they were in the main just wars, fought for independence, unity, and the liberation of others. If our Mexican and Indian wars contained elements of what would today be described as imperialism or colonialism, they went unnoticed in a world where colonialism and imperialism of a far more objectionable nature were rampant, as indeed they are today. If our economic expansion carried our products and methods to other lands, we felt, in the main rightly, that the advantages of those lands at least equaled those accruing to us. There was, we thought, no good reason for apologizing to a country for buying its sugar or fruit or coffee and selling it our machinery or wheat, or for developing its oil resources and then purchasing the oil.

Today, things are vastly different. The mood of many Americans is one of contrition. They don sackcloth and ashes and tell us that, far from expecting gratitude from those we help, we must make amends for the fact that we are in a position to help them. The obligation, it seems, is on our side, not theirs. We must wear penitent's garb because we have succeeded where they have failed. We must close our eyes to their many and patent internal injustices, their caste systems, their iron-bound social classes, their massacre of political opponents, their trampling and deporting of national and racial minorities, while at the same time we must magnify every mote in our own national eye until it becomes a beam.

In the sphere of international policy, it matters little that we have voluntarily rid ourselves of colonial possessions, granted independence to the Philippines, offered it (and had it refused) to Puerto Rico, respected the sovereign rights of smaller nations in our sphere of influence to the point of tolerating the insults, expropriations and aggressive intentions of a Fidel Castro. It matters little that the three wars we have waged since 1908 have all had as their precise purpose to help or liberate the victims of aggression and oppression.

Had we behaved like that great apostle of anti-imperialism and anticolonialism, the Soviet Union, we would by this time have swallowed up the Western Hemisphere equivalent of Lithuania, Latvia, Estonia, Poland, Hungary, Czechoslovakia, Romania, Albania, East Germany and part of Finland, and forcibly deported to other areas a million or so members of recalcitrant minorities. Following the example of that other great leader in the struggle against imperialism and colonialism, Communist China, we would have gone on to take over the equivalent of Tibet, North Korea and North Vietnam, and put the squeeze on the equivalent of India, Cambodia, Laos, South Vietnam and even Indonesia.

All this we have failed to do. Yet some people abroad charge us with imperialism, and other people at home, without exactly echoing the charge, advise us to beat our breasts.

Others want us to be apologetic for a so-called act of espionage. Even granting that any nation has a right to consider as territorial air space what is 60,000 feet above ground (well over the ten- or twelve-mile limit that any nation is entitled to at sea), the American of 1908 vintage would have been quick to reply that we would apologize only when, as and if other nations apologized for their countless acts of espionage on land, sea, and in the air. After all, we developed and paid for our own atom bomb; we did not steal it, through spies and bribed traitors, from other nations.

Most galling of all is the suggestion that we should be apologetically humble for having achieved, by our own efforts, the highest standard of living in history, one that other nations envy us and hope at some future time to achieve; and one that, incidentally, permits us to extend to them aid of all kinds. This suggestion reminds us of the *schnorrers,* or professional beggars, of the old Hebrew tradition, who claimed that those who gave them charity should be grateful to them because they, the beggars, afforded the donors the opportunity to carry out the religious obligation to give alms.

We can, and should be, sincerely humble and thankful to the God that many of our critics deny, both for our prosperity and for the possibility of helping others. But this emphatically does not mean that we must apologize for our wealth in the very act of giving it away. Least of all does it mean that we have to apologize to the recipients of our bounty for having it to give.

The American of 1908 took justifiable pride in his country, its progressive institutions, its system of government, its achievements, its wealth and its greatness. Let us not abdicate that just pride in deference to those who would like to see us humble ourselves before nations that are, and will continue to be, unable to humble us, much as they would like to!

The Issue of Foreign Aid

FOREIGN AID IS PROBABLY ONE OF THE MOST WIDELY misunderstood areas of government action, and the one in which the greatest misconceptions appear. Since foreign aid, both military and economic, costs the U. S. taxpayer close to five billion dollars a year, the question most frequently asked is: "Does not this huge sum weigh heavily upon the American economy, and is it not the major cause of red ink in our balance of international payments, and of the unrelenting pressure on our gold reserves?"

The answer is a qualified no. While over four billion dollars went out in foreign economic aid in 1964, less than one billion in gold actually left the country. Over three and a half billion dollars were used to purchase goods and services here. It was the goods and services, not the gold, that were exported. Our entire program of foreign economic aid meant a potential drain of little over 700 million on our gold stock. Too much, perhaps, and even the sums spent in the United States present a questionable feature that will be discussed later. But it is a far cry from being the sole, or even the major cause of our gold imbalance. The real major causes are the difference between what our tourists spend abroad and what foreign tourists spend here (over one and a half billion), and the difference between what American firms send out in the form of foreign investments and what our past investments bring back to us (nearly two billion).

As for foreign military aid, that has long been dwindling until now it amounts to less than a billion. How well spent is that sum is something for the military authorities to determine. Under any circumstances, it must be regarded as part of our defense budget, which few Americans, liberal or conservative, are willing to forgo, at least for the present. The only question involved is that of effectiveness, which in these days of high specialization is hardly for the layman to settle. If there is economic waste involved, it is for the military and the Congressional defense committees to do away with it.

Purely economic aid is different. It involves a philosophy of government, and there is a question of principle involved. Why foreign economic aid at all?

Such aid can be justified on only four grounds, each of which can legitimately be discussed by the layman: (1) Such aid is a charitable act whereby we relieve human misery abroad out of our own surplus resources; (2) foreign aid may serve to promote certain ends which the State Department judges beneficial to us in connection with our foreign policies; (3) it gains "goodwill" for us in the recipient nations, which again is beneficial to us; (4) it spurs the domestic economy by stimulating our production and exports, even if that extra production and those extra exports are entirely subsidized by their own beneficiaries, the American taxpayers. Note that point number 4 is generally muted and unpublicized, though it is doubtless very much in the back of the Administration's mind.

Point number 1, the alleviation of human misery abroad, is no doubt the most unselfish and praiseworthy. It is also the one that should regretfully be written off as not falling within the sphere of legitimate government activities, at home or abroad.

It is not the function of government to dole out charity to the needy, save perhaps on an emergency relief basis under circumstances of sudden disaster, such as an earthquake or a flood. The government's function is to promote the general welfare, not to relieve individual misery. A good case can be made out for quake and flood relief, in the same fashion that a public ambulance and a public hospital take immediate care of the victim of an automobile accident. *Chronic* poverty should not be subsidized or relieved by the government, though it should be the government's responsibility to see that it is prevented and abolished by wise policies. Its relief on a chronic basis properly pertains to charity-minded individuals and institutions, such as church agencies and foundations. If government steps into the charity field, it is compelling individuals to be charitable against their will, since government funds consist of tax moneys about contributing which the individual has no choice.

It is also argued that we should not attempt to relieve misery abroad while there is still much misery to relieve at home. This can be debated, but not on the plane of governmental philosophy. It is as wrong for the government to force me to give my money for the relief of poverty in American slums as for the relief of poverty in India. At best, it forces me to do good against my will, and robs of all its moral merit the contribution I might willingly make to the relief of misery.

Foreign economic aid can be and has been effectively used to promote our foreign policies and achieve certain desirable global ends. The Marshall Plan did much to speed the economic and military recovery of nations that it was to our advantage to set back on their feet. Here the big question is whether the aid is efficiently administered to produce maximum results with minimum expenditures. Another question is whether the aims and goals of such aid are invariably worthwhile from the American point of view.

This point is closely linked with that of building up goodwill abroad. Naturally, we stand to gain from having a foreign population feel kindly disposed or even grateful to us. But does economic aid achieve this goal?

There is considerable unrest among American taxpayers over the fact that nations that have been heavy recipients of our aid not only proclaim their neutrality or noncommittedness, but actively oppose our policies in the UN and elsewhere. Worse yet, they permit and even encourage public demonstrations against us at the slightest provocation, with attacks upon our embassies and consulates and burnings of USIA libraries. This has happened in Egypt, Algeria, Indonesia, Ghana and other countries too numerous to mention. It is not a series of sporadic incidents, nor can it be said that the demonstrations are spontaneous outbreaks on the part of a hotheaded minority, since in most of the countries where they have occurred the regime is of a dictatorial or semidictatorial type, and in a position to enforce a determined prohibition of such outbursts. Far too often the outbursts carry the imprint of government sanction and even encouragement. The question then legitimately arises in the American mind: "Shall we continue to subsidize and feed ingrates who bite the hand that feeds them?" If we do, we can no longer invoke the goodwill argument. We can only claim that regardless of the way the local population or its government feels about us and our aid, it suits our policies and furthers our interests to continue aiding these countries. The sign goes up: "Proceed at your own risk. You may be building up a potential enemy."

Is this a wise procedure? Should we shore up the economy of an Indonesia or an Egypt that may, when the chips are down, turn that same economy to the advantage of our potential foes? Ought we not rather to withhold aid in these cases, while bestowing it with an even more open hand on countries whose leadership we can count on? And ought we not to do so without regard for the form of government of the country that gets our aid? The democracies (in our sense of the term) are generally with us and behind us in principle, though they may occasionally differ on minor matters of procedure. For countries that are not democratically run, is there much to choose, ideologically, between Franco's Spain and Salazar's Portugal on the one hand, Tito's Yugoslavia and Nasser's Egypt on the other? The real difference is that Franco and Salazar are willing to be firmly committed to our side, Tito and Nasser are not. If we must bolster dictatorships as a matter of foreign policy, is it not better to bolster those that are with us than those that are against us? Would we not have been better off siding firmly with Chiang Kai-shek and Batista than flirting with Mao Tse-tung and Castro? Foreign policy must be realistic if it is to be foreign policy and not a flight into the wild blue yonder. Let us help our friends, even if we don't approve of everything they do, particularly since by helping them we may get them to mend their ways. Let us thwart, or at least not help, those who are either our avowed foes or lose no opportunity to inform us that they consider us on a par with or beneath our avowed foes.

Outside of realism, there remains the issue of popular gratitude, the accumulation of that elusive substance known as goodwill. When we help a country, we expect the population to know about it and be properly grateful, or at the very least friendly. Here the form taken by foreign aid, its method of distribution, the publicity that accompanies it, become important. Here we get the story of how a Peruvian Andean village, or a clump of Nigerian huts, turn everlastingly thankful because of the Peace Corpsman in their midst; how the setting up of an Alliance for Progress organization wins the undying gratitude of the people of Ecuador; how the shipment of free tractors to Iran and Pakistan turns the natives into lifelong friends of the United States, ready to resist all Communist blandishments.

It is difficult to evaluate episodes or generalize from them. It was brought out not too long ago that "the best-kept secret in the United Arab Republic appears to be the U.S. aid program—specifically, our vast shipments of surplus farm commodities to the tune of nearly one billion dollars in twelve years." The Nasser regime, it appears, permits no publicity whatsoever in this respect, while highlighting Soviet arms shipments, to be turned against Israel, and Aswan Dam aid. The U.S. markings are carefully removed from food packages, and practically no one in Egypt knows that we are making huge contributions to the population's survival.

This brings us squarely back to the issue of charity *vs.* foreign policy. The purest form of charity is anonymous, and if that is what we want, well and good. But foreign policy and even popular gratitude are determined by the group in power. If Nasser doesn't like us, it matters little how many Egyptians we save from starvation; they will never know it was we who saved them, and the next time there is a chance to take part in an anti-American demonstration, they will cheerfully participate.

The disadvantages of unpublicized foreign aid, even in the case of thoroughly friendly countries and governments, were borne in upon me by a personal experience. Traveling by bus from Rome to Naples in the summer of 1959, we made a luncheon stop at Cassino, with a visit to the famous abbey, scene of the American air bombings in World War Two. The abbey itself had been beautifully reconstructed, and the town, below, reduced to rubble in the course of the battle, had been completely rebuilt, with ultramodern housing for all the inhabitants.

Professionally, I was interested in viewing the 960 A.D. Testimonial Formulas of Monte Cassino, which are the first attested documents of the Italian language, and are kept in the library's archives. To my request that they be shown to me, the archivist replied with an obdurate no. The documents were kept under lock and key, he said, and could not be exhibited save on very special occasions. My credentials as Professor of Romance Philology at Columbia University availed me nothing. Neither did the obvious fact that I was a native Italian speaker. I could have carried my plea to a higher authority, but there was no time. The bus was due to leave for the town in ten minutes.

Discussing the incident over the luncheon table with a local priest, I remarked that there had seemed to be in the archivist's attitude a note of hostility. Could this be due to the fact that I was an American citizen, I wondered? The priest allowed that it might be so. "But why?" I persisted. "Well," he said, "you recall what happened here during the war." "Indeed I do," said I, "but it was a clear-cut case of military necessity. Anyhow, we did our best to make amends. Both the abbey and the town were rebuilt with American help." "Who told you that?" he almost snarled. "They were rebuilt by the Italian government and the Banco del Mezzogiorno; there was no American participation whatsoever!" "And where did they get the money?" I countered. "Have you ever heard of the Marshall Plan? The American government gave the Italian government some billions of dollars to reconstruct Italy and get her back on her feet, and the Italian government, with that money, financed a lot of worthy enterprises, the rebuilding of Cassino among them."

This was news to the priest. He had, in a vague sort of way, heard about the Marshall Plan, but it had not occurred to him to link it with what had gone on in his own area. Nor had the Italian government taken the trouble to publicize the fact. It had taken all the credit.

This was, in a sense, beneficial to us, because we wanted the Christian Democrat government to be popular among the masses, and thus offset the Communist drive for voters. At the same time, it would not have hurt to let those same voters know that America was helping, too. This, apparently, we had not insisted on. The net result was that the local population gave us full credit for the bombings, but no credit for the reconstruction.

This, then, seems to be the score to date on economic foreign aid:

It can be and has been effective in promoting certain policy aims. Whether these aims were invariably well thought out is questionable.

A great question mark attaches to the publicitarian, or goodwill, aspect of foreign aid. By and large, only a fraction of what could have been brought to pass has worked out.

Charity is highly meritorious, particularly when it is anonymous. But is such charity on a chronic, long-range international basis a government function?

One additional facet of foreign aid remains to be discussed. To what extent is foreign aid used to spur our own domestic economy, create employment, swell up production and export figures, get rid of our surpluses, and generally add to our internal prosperity? Officially, very little is said about this. Unofficially, any member of the foreign service will readily admit that this is one of the most important features of foreign aid. You cannot produce and export four billion dollars' worth of extra goods and services without adding to your employment, purchasing power, and general prosperity. Viewed from this angle, foreign aid becomes a major item of internal economic policy, highly beneficial in one sense. In another sense, it becomes a major inflationary factor in our economy, like farm subsidies, minimum wage laws, union featherbedding, and pork-barrel legislation, all things which go against a free market, but on which our economy seems to thrive, at least temporarily. It is all part of pump-priming, spending ourselves into prosperity, and owing it to ourselves.

A word of caution is in order. During the Fascist regime in Italy, the Italian government issued economic reports which showed amazing excesses of exports over imports, with implications of a booming economy and widespread prosperity. A breakdown of the figures revealed that the exports were mainly to Ethiopia and other parts of the Fascist empire, from which there was little if any return flow. The Italians could delude themselves into viewing this as an investment for the future. It just didn't happen to work out that way.

One wonders to what extent the impressive U.S. surplus of exports over imports may include parts of the four billion dollars, more or less, that represent goods and services produced here and shipped abroad as foreign aid. With us, of course, there is no question of investment, or expectation of an eventual return (American private investments abroad and returns from past investments appear as a separate item from imports and exports in our official figures). The question then is to what extent our impressive export figures represent cash transactions of the same economic nature as our imports, and to what extent they represent fictitious "exports" that are not paid for, save by ourselves to ourselves.

Even if foreign aid "exports" are kept carefully distinct from true exports, it is nevertheless a fact that they must be paid for, on the internal market, by the American taxpayer. If those amounts go to increase the purchasing power of the producers of goods and services, they reduce the purchasing power of the American taxpayer-consumer by a like amount. We are then faced with the customary redistribution of income, with the Federal Government, as usual, determining the redistribution.

It is perhaps more difficult to outline a sound conservative policy in the matter of foreign aid than in most other areas, by reason of the number and complexity of the factors involved.

It would be an oversimplification to take a traditional isolationistic stand and declare ourselves against all forms of foreign aid save in the purely military sphere. The questions at issue involve our foreign policy, our prestige and general image abroad, even our internal economy.

A few things, however, seem clear. Foreign economic aid should be carefully reexamined, item by item and country by country, to determine whether it is really in line with the goals of a foreign policy which should be highly realistic and aimed, first and foremost, at the best interests of the United States, and only secondarily at those of recipient nations. It should be reduced where possible, never squandered with a free and reckless hand, as it too often has been in the past.

Save for sudden emergencies, it should never be based on charitable ideals, or even the recipient's need, however dire. On the other hand, there is no reason why the government should not encourage churches, private agencies and private foundations to assist in the relief of poverty and misery abroad, in their own way and on as broad a scale as possible. Americans are traditionally charitable, openhanded and openhearted. There is no doubt that they will respond to appeals, as witnessed by CARE and kindred initiatives. Private institutions also have their own way of distributing aid in such a fashion that the recipients know where it is coming from. There is all the difference in the world, psychologically, between the U. S. Government granting the government of a foreign nation one hundred million dollars to use as it chooses (there is little doubt that a good deal of it falls into the wrong hands), and a private organization which functions on the spot and knows what the immediate needs of the community are.

As a matter of general principle, official aid should be withheld from those countries and governments which display attitudes of opposition or downright hostility and animosity against us. If they want to hate us as capitalistic, colonialistic aggressors, that is their privilege; but they should not be allowed to hold out one hand for a loaf of American bread while with the other they tear down our flag to trample on it.

For the uncommitted, neutralistic nations, requests for foreign aid should be viewed with a jaundiced eye. Let them feel free to apply to Russia or China if they feel they can get a better deal that way. The friendship of certain countries, like that of certain people, is sometimes a liability rather than an asset. Unless there is strong reason to the contrary, let our opponents enjoy the liability.

Our avowed and sincere friends we should back to the limit. Nor should we worry unduly about their internal form of government. As between two dictators, better one who likes us and hates Communism than one who has Communistic leanings, despises us, and misses no opportunity to let us know it.

It would be wise, particularly in connection with foreign aid, to preach less democracy abroad and let democracy work by example. We have a form of government and a social and economic system which, with all their avowed imperfections, are nevertheless among the most satisfactory on earth. They are open for all to see and study. Unlike some of our critics, there is little if anything that we strive to conceal, whether it be racial strife in the South or crime waves in the North, election scandals in one locality or graft and corruption elsewhere. But under our system, imperfect as it is, we have achieved things that the entire world envies us—a larger measure of personal freedom, initiative and opportunity than is found elsewhere, standards of living and material prosperity that are hard to duplicate. These things speak for themselves. People who come to our land and return to their own, American films, radio and TV, industrial concerns that do business abroad, spread the gospel of American methods and viewpoints and American democracy far more effectively than all our government agencies put together. It is not the height of wisdom for us to link our aid, where it is given, to the reform of internal government structures in the recipient lands, save only insofar as those reforms may help the recipients to help themselves. Even internationally, there is such a thing as a "Mother, I'd rather do it myself!" attitude. In more cases than we care to admit, the existing political structure of a country is the one best suited for its present conditions. As those conditions change in the economic and educational spheres, there will almost inevitably be a change in the political structure, that will bring it more in line with our own ideals. We should not attempt to use foreign aid as a weapon of political reform, though it may be a useful tool for economic and educational development.

We are here reminded of an American military commander in a southern Italian area who insisted that there should be immediate and free elections. When assured by the local political leaders that such an election would be almost surely won by the Communists, he was equally insistent that they should not win. Fortunately, the Italian politicians were at least as skilled in the art of manipulating a "free" election as are the leaders of certain Chicago wards, and everything came out all right.

In conclusion:

1. For best image results, replace government-to-government aid with people-to-people aid wherever possible.
2. Insist upon appropriate publicity where the aid is still government-to-government.
3. Refuse aid to those who openly hate and oppose us.
4. Cut down aid to those who can't make up their minds whether they prefer us or our opponents.
5. Extend full aid to those who like and support us.
6. Link aid to realistic foreign policy, not to political ideologies.

I am the first to admit that these are not clear-cut solutions. But foreign aid, like foreign policy generally, does not admit of clear-cut solutions. Situations are forever shifting, and must be handled as they arise, while in foreign aid, as in foreign policy, only half the power of determination is ours, with the other half quite properly pertaining to the nation with which we are dealing at the moment.

The Consent of the Governed

IN THE MIDST OF ALL OUR PRESENT CONCERN FOR THE world's "fledgling nations" and the preservation or extension of democratic forms of government to them and to others, we are sometimes forced to wonder whatever happened to an older American slogan popularized by an idealist of an older generation, "self-determination for small nations."

Regardless of the fact that Wilson's formula was only exceptionally applied at the end of World War One, and that where it was applied it ultimately led to unsatisfactory results (the carving up of the Austro-Hungarian Empire, for instance, with the consequent rise of small nations such as Czechoslovakia, Hungary, Yugoslavia, Romania, which, being small and disunited, proved an easy prey for the Nazis first, the Communists later), there was inherent merit in the proposition that clearly defined national groups should determine for themselves their future affiliations and forms of government.

The plebiscite system had fairly extensive application in the nineteenth century, despite the fact that that was the era of "imperialism" par excellence. Our imperialistic ancestors on occasion would decree that the population of a given area be polled, and its wishes at least considered. Even where the outcome had been prearranged, as in Italy's cession of Nice and Savoy to France, or where the plebiscite served merely to ratify a military conquest, this lip service to the democratic process had its own peculiar merits, for it set up the will of the people as a theoretical, ideal goal.

What goes on today, even under the auspices of such an august international body as the UN, is the complete negation of this ideal principle. De Gaulle promised the Algerians, both of French and Arab origin, a plebiscite to determine the status of the country; actually, that status was settled by direct negotiations between the French government and the Algerian rebel leaders. The fact that the outcome would probably have been the same still does not justify the bypassing of the democratic process. The status of Cyprus and Katanga was similarly settled, after long and bloody conflicts. Most recent examples of massive unconcern for the popular will are Goa, West Irian and Cuba.

In the case of the first, Portugal claimed that the inhabitants were full-fledged Portuguese citizens, with all the rights and privileges of Portuguese citizenship, and that they wanted to retain that status. India claimed that the enclave was on Indian soil, and the people were Indians. It occurred to neither, nor to the higher councils of a body that claims to be supra-national, to poll the Goans and find out how they stood. Instead, India went to war, overwhelmed the small local Portuguese garrison, and seized Goa, proclaiming it a part of India. The same reluctance to find out what the people concerned want appears in the Kashmir controversy between India and Pakistan. Apparently India, the great peace-loving nation, believes in peace and democracy so long as its own interests are not involved, in recourse to violence and seizure by force of arms where they are. It is only fair to point out that the imperialistic powers of the nineteenth century shared this view and methodology.

Another great peace-lover, Indonesia, believed that West Irian (the western area of the island of New Guinea) should belong to it. Here there was not even India's justification of racial and linguistic affinity, for the inhabitants of West Irian are black Papuans, not brown Indonesians. The Netherlands, holding the area, declared in favor of a plebiscite. This offer was turned down in favor of military action. Fortunately for all concerned, there was no economic value to West Irian, so the Dutch shrugged their shoulders and let Indonesia have its way. Not a word of censure from the UN concerning this act of imperialistic aggression. At any rate, it is doubtful if the backward Papuans would have had any idea of what a plebiscite would have been about.

With Cuba, the situation was different. Both bad, corrupt, American-loving Batista and Castro the liberator had promised the Cuban people a free election. When Castro took control, he reneged on his promises. He has been in power for years, but there hasn't been a trace of a free election yet. Those American liberals who made a hero of Castro now realize that, dictator for dictator, we might as well have continued with one who liked us rather than one who likes the Russians. Again, not a chirp out of the UN.

But the UN chirps plenty when it is a matter of condemning Portugal for holding on to Angola, or South Africa for not sending its three million whites back to Europe, like the one and a half million European Algerians, and turning the country over to the more numerous Bantu, who in this particular case are no more indigenous to the area than are the Boers, having invaded it in the seventeenth and eighteenth centuries and practically exterminated the aboriginal Hottentot-Bushman tribes. The African-Asian bloc of nations are very vocal about imperialism and aggression, but only when it suits their preferences and prejudices.

The consent of the governed is very important for areas like Kenya and the Congo, Ghana and Niger, Morocco and Tunisia, not at all important for Hungary and Poland, East Germany and Czechoslovakia, Estonia and Lithuania. Could this be racial prejudice in reverse?

There are many Americans who view the UN, its present composition, its functioning as a world government in embryo, with a decidedly jaundiced eye. At one time this attitude could have been ascribed to an isolationistic mentality and a feeling of indifference for what goes on in the world.

Today this is no longer true. The critical attitude of

anti-UN Americans is based squarely upon the lack of satisfactory performance by that supposedly international body, by its approvals and condemnations based not on principles of justice, equity and freedom, but on neo-nationalistic tendencies on the part of too many member nations that are decidedly immature.

Who is responsible for the admission of so many immature nations? That is a very good question, but one to which we unfortunately do not have the full and complete answer. We should be happy to get one from our great organs of public information.

At any rate, the UN as at present constituted is a rather hopeless hodgepodge of real and make-believe nations, of countries that have political maturity, even if they do not all subscribe to an ideal system of government, and other countries that describe themselves as democracies, but where the effective power rests with a handful of educated people, as well as of countries that believe in popular rule and countries that believe in absolute government.

Perhaps the UN would be best dissolved and replaced by what a political writer of the prewar period described as the "Union of the Free"—a bloc of those nations, white, black, yellow and brown, that truly believe in the consent of the governed and the rights of the individual. An aristocratic concept perhaps, but at least one that would assure Americans of survival among equals.

Who Is Responsible?

IN ONE OF HIS COLUMNS, EDGAR ANSEL MOWRER protests about the use of "we" in such statements as "We older people have made a mess of world affairs and should now shut up and leave matters to the younger generation."

"Who's we, anyhow?" he inquires. At the most, it was "they" who made the errors, though we all pay the price for those errors. But who are "they"?

In an earlier presidential race, candidate Kennedy lashed out with a body blow at his opponent: "U.S. prestige today is at an all-time low!" he claimed. There was a logical counter for candidate Nixon. "Yes, and when did it all start?" The discussion would have gone on to show that the original errors were made under Roosevelt, compounded under Truman; that the sell-out of Yalta and other similar meetings with Stalin, followed by the spirit of Potsdam and "Good old Joe," followed by the lack of support for Chiang Kai-shek in China, followed by the sabotaging of victory in Korea, could only lead to the subsequent and consequent errors committed under Eisenhower, who gave us an armistice in Korea, the Suez fiasco in Egypt, the Russian tanks in Hungary, Ho Chi Minh in Vietnam, Castro in Cuba.

Instead, candidate Nixon, preoccupied with defending Eisenhower's record, chose to fight with one hand tied behind his back, claiming that American prestige abroad had never been higher. He lost that election.

Two sayings come to mind. One is "The evil that men do lives after them." The other one is in the form of a children's jingle that starts: "For want of a nail the shoe was lost," and goes on to the loss of the horse, the rider, the message, the battle, the war and the nation.

In foreign policy, we have made one mistake after another. "Mistake," of course, is a charitable interpretation.

There was no need for concessions to Stalin during the war. Stalin had far more to fear from the Nazis than we did, and he knew it. We could have insisted on the liberation of all of Europe, instead of giving up the eastern half to Communism. We could have taken all of Germany and reunified it (or not reunified it) to suit ourselves. We could have occupied Berlin, Prague and Budapest. We could have insisted that the Russians stay out of the Japanese war, of which they had wanted no part until Japan was ready to capitulate. Why didn't we? No one knows.

Later on, we could at least have stopped the Chinese

Reds at the line of the Yangtze, by sending some real naval forces, not just the two British gunboats that had to run the gauntlet, up that river. I recall making the suggestion to a liberal friend, and the look of shocked surprise that overspread his face. "Oh, we couldn't do that!" he protested. Why not?

Some people had the idea of taming Mao Tse-tung and the Chinese Reds, just as later they had the idea of turning Castro into a tower of democracy. Neither worked out.

We had our second chance at the Chinese Reds when they joined the North Korean aggressors. We could have unleashed our bombs on their bases beyond the Yalu, and Chiang Kai-shek on their southern flank. We preferred a stalemate. This time the blame went to our allies, because Korea was, after all, a UN police action, not an American enterprise. Then we wondered why our soldiers in Korea were confused, demoralized, and an easy prey for Communist propaganda. They had foolishly thought they were risking their lives to win a war, as America had always won all wars, not just to hold a parallel.

The story continues with an anticolonialism policy that resulted in Dien Bien Phu and a divided Vietnam, Sukarno (the self-proclaimed Lenin of Southeast Asia) in Indonesia, Nasser in Egypt, Nkrumah in Ghana, Ben Bella and Boumedienne in Algeria. There was the Bay of Pigs in Cuba, the invasion to overthrow Castro that apparently had the support of our CIA but not of our Air Force, withdrawn at the last moment because "somebody" was afraid of the bad impression it would make on the Latin nations. So we later had Russian missiles in Cuba. There was a teetering that has cost us or may cost us Vietnam, Cambodia and Laos. There is an "Alliance for Progress" that proves only that the more aid we give the more they dislike us. There is an American UN policy that antagonizes good allies who are also founding members of that organization, Belgium and France and Holland and Portugal and South Africa, in favor of "nations" that are either uncommitted or hostile, and that should not have been admitted for another fifty years at least, until they had had time to grow up.

After each one of these mistakes, after the loss of each new land to Communism, the official attitude is: "Too bad! Something went wrong! Well, better luck next time!" So far, we have been lucky enough to have had a next time.

One never gets to find out exactly who is responsible for each mistake. Ultimate responsibility rests with the President who happens to be in the White House, but the President has to be advised. By whom?

There are countries where the punishment for "errors" is the same as for treason. Fortunately, we are not that kind of country.

But is it too much to ask that the people responsible for the errors get out, and let someone else have a try at running the foreign policy? Or must we go on from one "error" to the next until we are worn down to the point where nobody trusts, respects or fears us, and the Communists take us over by default?

IV

Taxation and Finance

Your Income Tax

THE EVILS OF THE PROGRESSIVE INCOME TAX HAVE BEEN described and discussed at length by many writers. They can be grouped under two general headings: inefficiency, economic waste, and the destruction of initiative on the one hand; basic unconstitutionality and opposition to our fundamental philosophy and principles of government on the other.

Both angles need to be reexamined and reevaluated. In addition, we are faced with the need of presenting suitable and realistic substitutes. In a modern civilization, with an international situation such as we are confronted with, it is not realistic to say that the Federal Government (or the state governments, for that matter) should economize to the point where the revenue from the income tax can be dispensed with. There is no doubt that very extensive economies could and should be practiced. But when all is said and done, we shall still have federal and state budgets, of a thoroughly legitimate variety, that will call for between one-half and three-quarters of present appropriations. Our destructive criticism of something that ought to be abolished on moral and legal grounds should therefore be accompanied by proposals designed to raise for our various forms of government, federal, state and local, the revenues they need to carry out their legitimate functions and activities.

Lastly, we must squarely face the possibility that the institution of the income tax, basically uneconomic and unconstitutional as it is, may have become so deeply rooted in the mores and thought-habits of our population that it will be impossible to eradicate it, at least for the time being, and until a new generation has come to voting age that will have been nurtured in the principles of true freedom and individualism. We must therefore also present a program of reform and relief that envisages the survival, at least temporarily, of the income tax as an institution and a way of life, and aims at doing away with its most unjust and pernicious features and consequences.

The following four essays are designed to present the four facets of the income tax problem we have described.

What the Income Tax Does to Our Economy

WHEN THE INCOME TAX AMENDMENT WAS PASSED, IT WAS pointed out by some of its opponents that it might result in as much as 3 or 4 percent of a person's income being taxed away from him. What has happened since is common knowledge.

In 1945, I pointed out in an article that in comparison with 1941, my food bill had risen over 100 percent; clothing, recreation and miscellaneous 30 to 50 percent; rent, gas, electricity and telephone practically nothing (thanks to irrational rent control and supervision of the utilities); and my income tax from $38 to $1,900 a year, or 5,000 percent. I therefore labeled the federal income tax as the most violently inflationary of all the forces tending to drive the inflationary spiral upward. I added:

"The income tax drives me and all the millions of others who work with their hands or brains to seek ways and means of maintaining our living standards and at the same time paying those taxes. We can do this in one of two ways: by adding to our work so as to earn more income, or by demanding higher rates of compensation for the work we do. Since the first device is restricted by the availability of work and by physical and mental limitations, higher rates of compensation are universally sought. This means higher prices for the farmer's products and the worker's labor. But higher prices have to be passed on to the consumer, who happens to be pretty much the same farmer and the same worker. Higher living costs are then superimposed on taxes to create a demand for more price or pay boosts. If the price or pay boosts are refused, we have deliberate lags in production, black markets, and strikes, leading to more production cuts. Employers and labor unions fight fierce battles over which shall come first—the higher price or the higher wage. The real villain of the plot goes unnoticed. He is what started the inflation spiral on its upward way—your income tax!

"Everybody tries to get everybody else to pay his income tax. The farmer figures it in the price of his product and passes it on to the wholesaler, who adds his own income tax and passes it on to the retailer, who sends it on to the consumer with still another income tax boost. The industrial worker figures his income tax in the pay boost he demands of his employer. The manufacturer slaps his on to his product. The physician or dentist who treats you adds 20 to 30 percent to his bill because he has to pay a big income tax. Private schools and universities boost fees to their students because they want to raise the salaries of their teachers and administrators, who clamor that they can't live on what they used to get now that the Federal Government siphons off one-fourth of it. If I am asked to do a special job of translating, revision or criticism for a certain fee, I must lop off one-third from the proffered figure to reach the real amount of compensation I am going to receive.

"In every phase of the nation's activity, the income tax is there, strangling initiative and boosting costs. In the case of things that go through half a dozen hands, like food, the income tax is probably responsible for all of the 100 percent rise, because each handler must add at least 20 percent of his former normal profit to take care of his tax bill.

"The government would like to see each citizen absorb his own income tax. This is visionary. People brought up on the profit motive simply aren't built that way. Nor would it be economically desirable. If everyone cut down his living standards, as he would have to do in order to absorb his income tax, many products would go unbought and unsold, the nation's economic activity would slow down, and widespread unemployment and depression would result. Americans prefer inflation to depression."

The steeply progressive feature of the income tax tends to stifle initiative. As matters stand today, and with a few variations for single and married taxpayers, income above $30,000 a year is taxed at rates close to 50 percent. State income taxes must be added where they exist, with the federal tax nondeductible. This amounts to practical confiscation, reducing a $200,000 income to about $50,000 minus state tax. It makes a joke of big salaries. It is inflationary in the sense that a concern which wants to give an executive an actual income boost of $10,000 must give him a $50,000 salary increase. The story is told of a big business executive who turned down a $200 suit offered him by his tailor on the ground that he couldn't afford it. "I would have to make $2,000 extra to buy that suit" was the way he put it.

If I am offered a piece of work for which there is a $100 compensation, I must figure it this way: since this extra $100 goes into my income at my top bracket, 34 percent of it goes to the Federal Government, 10 percent to the state; but since the state tax is deductible from the federal, I pay only about 6 percent. The job that apparently pays me $100 pays in reality only $60. Is it worth my while? If this same job is offered to Governor Rockefeller, at his top bracket of 91 plus 10 percent, he would disburse 101 percent in taxes, were it not that he would have the same federal deductibility for his state tax. At any rate, the combined taxes would amount to $97, leaving him $3. I doubt that you could get him to accept.

The destruction of incentive goes all the way from the movie star with her one million dollars for a picture, of which she may perhaps retain $100,000 if her lawyer is good at figuring deductions and making them stick, to the laborer in the 20 to 30 percent bracket, who might feel inclined to do overtime for $3 an hour, but not for $2.25.

Inflation is a matter of personal taste. Some people thrive on it. Incentive, or the lack thereof, is likewise a personal matter. Many people like to work for the love of the game. What is not subject to taste or discussion is the infinite waste of time and labor to which every taxpayer is subjected by the income tax. Even the low-income man who uses the short form, takes the standard deduction, and relies on his withholdings to take care of his tax obligations must figure out at the end of the year whether he owes the government or vice versa. For anyone compelled to use the long form, there is mental stress and strain that often takes up the better part of a working week when the final return has to be made out, plus the keeping of endless records of income and legitimate deductions. Nor will it avail supporters of the income tax as a way of life to argue that you can hire an accountant to do the paper work. You must still supply the accountant with all the relevant figures and records.

A Gallup Poll should be taken to determine the amount of time expended by the average man on his income tax figures and records. This, multiplied by the number of taxpayers in the United States, would no doubt give us an astronomical figure, running into the billions or trillions of man-hours per year—hours which many of us could devote to far more productive pursuits.

Add to this the economic waste represented by the paper and supplies used by the government, business and individuals in producing, filing and storing all the infinite records connected with the income tax, particularly when these records have to be duplicated by and for the state, and it will readily be seen that the income tax is about as uneconomic a procedure as could be devised for the purpose of supplying the government with the revenues it needs.

Another baneful feature of the income tax is that many, not to say most, of our activities have to be predicated upon it. The income tax colors our transactions and the thinking that is connected with them, forces us to do things we would not normally do and refrain from doing things that should be done. A given transaction, if placed in a certain period, may be taxed at a different rate. We must therefore either buy or sell a house, a block of shares, a piece of property at an economically wrong time, or be penalized by taxation. My better judgment may tell me to sell a stock now, but if I hold it another month I will pay half the tax. But holding it another month may lead to a considerable financial loss. Nevertheless, I am impelled to hold on by the tax feature, often to my own detriment. All other things being equal, I am forced to prefer working and living in one state rather than another, because one state has an income tax, the other has not. I must anticipate, or put off, making a necessary expenditure because my tax rate or liability next year will be lower, or higher, than it is now. I am forced to resort to contracts with unusual features designed to cut down my tax liability. Whereas the American of the past could invariably judge a situation, an offer, an opportunity, on its own merits, the American of the present more often than not has to judge it on the way it will affect his tax bill.

This is uneconomic, wasteful, harmful, unjust. It puts a premium on an item that is unconnected with the activity itself. It makes of us a nation of tax-dodgers, watching the line between tax evasion and tax avoidance, subordinating our logical thinking to the blind factor of the income tax.

Possibly the worst feature of the income tax in its far-reaching consequences is the item of tax deductibility. It leads us to make contributions that we would not normally make, and withhold our support from activities that would otherwise receive it. On the one hand, it lends itself to mental, moral and financial dishonesty, even when we stay within the law. On the other, it has led to the creation and growth of huge foundations, with vast financial power, that tend to be policy-making and influence even the government, and that are responsible to no one but the people who have gained control of them. While it is undoubtedly true that these foundations support many worthwhile causes, it is equally true that they often finance activities that ought not to be supported—at any rate, not at the taxpayer's expense. Every dollar that goes into contributions is a dollar taken out of the pocket of the individual taxpayer, who is forced to make up the difference to the government. In the final analysis, religious, charitable and scientific-educational institutions, being of a private nature, should be privately endowed. As matters stand, they are partly endowed by taxpayers who have no faith, interest or voice in what these institutions are doing.

It is sometimes claimed that such organizations would founder without the tax-deductible feature. But many existed before the income tax, and were supported by people who really believed in them, to the extent of contributing to their support altogether out of their own pockets. They were not supported out of the pocket of the community at large.

What the individual (or the business organization) does in the matter of claiming deductions is between his own conscience and the Internal Revenue bureau that examines his return. Not even the most sanguine upholder of the income tax will deny that many deductions go through unchallenged that ought not to. At any rate, the mood fostered by the deduction, even in the most conscientious of us, is: "What can I get away with in the matter of deductions?" This is an unhealthy moral state of affairs, and tends to be reflected in other fields.

Of all the forms of taxation devised, the income tax is the most harmful, both to the nation's economic structure and to the nation's moral fiber.

The Power to Tax Is the Power to Destroy

THAT THE PERSONAL INCOME TAX IS CONTRARY TO THE spirit of the original Constitution will not be seriously denied by anyone who cares to reread Part 4 of Section 9.

But the Constitution also provides for its own amendment, and the Sixteenth Amendment was passed in full accord with the prescribed procedure. There is little doubt that if we want to get rid of the income tax, we shall have to do so by another, repealing amendment.

But there is another constitutional principle involved in the individual income tax—the right of the individual to life, liberty and the pursuit of happiness, all of which are infringed by the principle of the income tax. "The power to tax is the power to destroy" appears in one of our earliest Supreme Court decisions. The power to lay a direct tax upon the individual is tantamount to giving the government (federal, state or local) the power to destroy that individual. Since our philosophy of government is based squarely on the idea that government exists for the individual, and not the individual for the government, this power should be removed.

Strangely, the archenemies of our philosophy of government and way of life have grasped this principle far better and more promptly than we have. Lenin's advocacy (for nations that have not yet attained the Communist paradise) of a steeply graduated income tax clearly shows that he viewed such a tax as a step (possibly the major step) in reaching his objective of wiping out of existence government by, of and for the individual, and replacing it with government by, of and for the all-powerful state.

If we ever took the trouble to listen carefully to what our enemies have to say (which we do not, as witnessed by the widespread ignorance that prevailed in the Western democracies concerning Hitler's principles and intentions, so clearly outlined in *Mein Kampf)*, this might have been enough to put us on our guard. As a matter of principle, anything that is advocated, particularly for us, by our enemies should be at the very least suspect as designed for our undoing (note that Communist countries generally eschew the income tax, and raise their revenue by what amounts to a huge invisible sales tax).

We utterly failed to view with alarm not only Lenin's clear pronouncement, but even such well-meant and widely publicized proposals as Mrs. Eleanor Roosevelt's suggestion, at the time of the war, that all personal incomes should be held down to a maximum of $25,000 a year, or Harry Hopkins' more brutally expressed views in his *American Magazine* article "*You* Will Be Drafted!" and his slogan about taxing, spending and electing. The most charitable thing that can be said of such suggestions is that their proponents were stupidly playing the game of the Communists. If the people of America ever want out-and-out Communism, all they have to do is to vote for it by a series of constitutional amendments. They do not have to be led into it by the nose by so-called liberal thinkers.

The income tax, federal, state or local, is not merely an uneconomic way of raising the revenue the governments need, one that puts an unnecessary burden upon government, business and individuals alike. It is also an instrument of policy designed to subvert our philosophy of government and our way of life. Only those who are blind can fail to see this.

More years ago than we care to count, there was widespread rejoicing over the fact that Al Capone, whom the authorities of the state of Illinois were powerless to convict for his many crimes, was finally brought to book by the Federal Government on charges not of murder, rapine or extortion, but of income tax evasion.

The occasion was hardly one for joy. Had the people stopped to reflect, they would have seen in it confirmation of the fact that the Sixteenth Amendment had saddled them forevermore with a central government that could henceforth delve into the most private details of their lives and deprive them of their liberties at its own whim. That this power, in the Capone instance, was exercised in a worthy cause is irrelevant as far as the principle at stake is concerned.

Before the enactment of the Sixteenth Amendment, the Federal Government could enter into the life of the individual only to the extent that the individual chose to renounce the protection of his own state in order to indulge in interstate activities, or to purchase commodities, none of them essential, subject to federal excises or tariffs. The

Sixteenth Amendment firmly settled the Federal Government not upon the states, but upon the individual.

It has been claimed sporadically, since 1913, that the Federal Government can, and on occasion does, use its power of taxation over the individual in a harmful and unjust fashion, and that the federal income tax has been used not merely as a revenue-raising device, but as an instrument of internal policy to favor some classes and persons and oppress others. We need not go into instances of New Deal and Fair Deal badgering of people and corporations through the income tax. The issue is not one of episode, but of principle. As matters stand, the individual has no true legal recourse against confiscation and liquidation at the hands of the Federal Government.

This was not the intention of the founding fathers, who wished the central government to exert its carefully circumscribed authority not upon the individual, but upon the states. Regardless of interpretations placed upon the Sixteenth Amendment by the Supreme Court, it is unconstitutional in its very essence, since it deprives the individual of his right to life, liberty and the pursuit of happiness. What has happened to the very rich, who have seen over 90 percent of their income disappearing into the jaws of the federal treasury, can in principle happen to the man in the very lowest income brackets. In fact, it has begun to happen.

There are some who advocate that with the repeal of the federal income tax this form of taxation be left to the states. From the standpoint of constitutional and philosophical principle, does it make any difference whether the power to destroy the individual is wielded by a federal or by a state government? Or, for that matter, even by a local government? Are state bureaucrats more sacrosanct, or considerate, than federal ones?

The principle at stake is the freeing of the individual from the oppressive power of government, which, as things stand, deprives us of our liberties and makes us subject to the will and whim of bureaucrats. Whether or not this power is exercised at all times, whether it is exercised in greater or lesser degree, whether it is exercised by the federal or the state government, is irrelevant. The power to tax, exercised directly and inescapably upon the individual, is the power to destroy that individual. We live only by grace of an all-powerful government as long as the Sixteenth Amendment and state statutes based on its model continue on our statute books.

What Can We Substitute for the Income Tax?

THE QUESTION OF EXPEDIENCY IS BROUGHT UP EVERY time the federal income tax is questioned. How else will the government raise the revenues it needs to carry on its multiform activities, particularly in the sphere of national defense?

There are forms of taxation that raise revenues without tampering with the individual's private life and private affairs. Excises, sales taxes, road and bridge tolls are only three of them. One can purchase items and services subject to such forms of taxation or refrain from them, thereby safeguarding his right of free choice. Above all, one can purchase such items and services without having to reveal to an inquisitive bureaucrat all the details of his economic and even of his personal life.

The argument that such forms of taxation bear most heavily upon those least able to pay is arrant nonsense. The rich spend far more than the poor. Items subject to these forms of taxation have in the past been carefully selected, with a view to sparing those least able to pay. These forms of taxation have been in existence for decades without harmful results. It is merely a question of studying, extending and applying them.

The only forms of taxation that even distantly parallel the income tax in their effect upon the relationship between individual and government are the personal property tax (a tax upon what you, as an individual, own) and those outmoded varieties of poll tax where you are taxed not for the privilege of voting, but for the privilege of existing.

All other forms of taxation leave you, as an individual, free from government supervision, control, inspection and interference. A real estate tax is something you pay for the privilege of owning real property; this you do not have to own. If you live in a rented house or apartment, you may in effect be paying a real estate tax, but only indirectly and without direct compulsion upon you from the government. Excises, sales taxes, road and bridge tolls, are all things you can conceivably and lawfully refrain from paying by the simple expedient of not using the objects or facilities subject to such taxes and tolls. Even where these are paid directly by you, there is no government pressure exerted upon you as an individual. The payment of an excise, a sales tax, a toll, is highly impersonal. And you have, in most instances, alternative choices. But the only alternative to paying an income tax is to have no income, and this means starving to death. Other forms of taxation do not imply that the government is reaching out to you as an individual and taking possession of you; it is only reaching out to the things you may desire to buy, possess or use.

Everyone is familiar with the principle and practice of indirect taxation, because everyone has experienced and is experiencing it. We pay taxes indirectly every time we purchase a package of cigarettes, a gallon of gasoline, a bottle of beer. The government, federal, state or local, imposes the tax not on us as individuals, but on the product we wish to acquire. The tax is paid by the manufacturer, included in the price of the product, and passed on by him to the retailer, who then passes it on to the consumer. It is of interest to note that prior to the passage of the Sixteenth Amendment the Federal Government derived over 90 percent of its revenue from such forms of indirect taxation as liquor and tobacco excises and import duties. This meant that the individual never had direct contact with the Federal Government and could not, by definition, violate a federal tax law. If he wanted the product, he paid the tax as part of the packaged price. If he objected to the tax, he could refrain from purchasing the product. It was as simple as that.

This principle and practice safeguarded the individual's freedom from government at the same time that it supplied the government with the revenue it needed. It made us a nation of truly free individuals.

While the individual had no contact with the government in this procedure, the manufacturer or retailer did. It was his function to collect the revenue for the government and pay it to the government. But the manufacturer, importer or retailer, even if he operated a one-man business, was not functioning as an individual, but as a concern. He sought the privilege of doing business among the community, which is not a basic right of the individual, but rather a form of social contract. In return for this privilege, he collected and passed on the government's revenue. No one forced him to be in business, and he entered into the arrangement of his own free will and with his eyes open. His position was, in a sense, similar to that of one who seeks a license to hunt or fish on public property.

The principle of hidden taxation is what safeguards the individual from contact with and harassment by the government. The principle begins to weaken in the directly imposed sales tax, but is basically still operative and intact. As an individual, you are not forced to buy the item subject to sales tax, and you still have no direct contact with the government. Such forms of taxation as the real estate tax bring you in direct touch with the government, but by your own choice. Only the income tax places the hand of government firmly on your shoulder and makes you a subject rather than a citizen.

The problem, then, is to devise a form of taxation so broadly based that all will pay it, more or less in proportion to their means, as they at present pay the income tax; that will bring in as much revenue as the government needs to carry on its legitimate activities; that will be as relatively simple and easy to administer and collect as are present-day excises; and that will break the stranglehold the government has at present on the individual, leaving only a formal contact between the government and the organization, corporate or otherwise, that deliberately chooses to make itself the government's tax collector as part of a freely sought and accepted contract authorizing it to do business with the collectivity which the government represents.

For a broadly based federal tax, which would in effect be paid by everyone, roughly in proportion to his means and ability to pay, yet would not directly affect the individual or lay him open to the threat of destruction by government, one might suggest that all firms organized to do business of any kind, whether on a giant corporate or puny personal basis, be made subject to a single disbursement tax based on a percentage of their total annual disbursements and expenditures. Such disbursements would include payrolls, purchases of goods and materials, dividends paid to stockholders, interest paid on indebtedness, royalties paid to authors, pension and annuity payments by insurance companies, advertising, rent, even telephone and utilities bills—in short, everything that goes on the expenditure side of a firm's ledger. The disbursement tax would not be reportable to or by, or be recoverable by the individual or firm to which the disbursement is made, even if it is passed on (as it undoubtedly would be) in the form of lower disbursements (wages, dividends, interest, royalties, etc.) or higher prices. The individual, as an individual, would pay nothing, but the tax would be reflected in the amounts he would receive as income, whether from salary or wages, pensions or annuities, dividends or interest, rents or royalties; or in the prices he would pay for the goods and services he buys.

As matters stand at present, an employing firm pays a corporate income tax on its profits. Its worker pays a personal income tax on his salary or wages. Its stockholder pays a personal income tax on his dividends, its bondholder on his interest, its suppliers on their profits from what they sell it. Adoption of this proposal would mean that the employing firm would pay a single disbursement tax on its payrolls, dividends, interest on bonded or other indebtedness, purchases of power and materials, advertising; passing on the tax, indirectly and unofficially, to its workers, stockholders, suppliers, purchasers, creditors, and customers.

All business firms, all individuals engaged in organized business, big or small, normally and as a matter of course keep a record of income and expenditures. The single disbursement tax would be extremely easy to figure out and to check up on. The burden of keeping records would be lifted from the individual as an individual. The hand of government would still extend over business, commerce and industry, as it does now. But it would be lifted from the individual as such.

This type of tax would to some extent be deflationary, and a reasonable measure of deflation is what we need. It would tend to make business administrations economy-minded, and this, too, would be good. It would drastically reduce amounts now spent on promotion and advertising, and particularly the inflated expense account, since the tax would be in direct ratio to amounts spent (more often wasted) on the theory that if you don't spend it it goes to the government anyway.

But the incentive to make and show a profit would be enhanced. Business would be penalized by taxation not for efficiency, as it is now, but for inefficiency in not knowing how to keep its expenditures down and its gross profits up. Legitimate advertising and promotion would still go on; but they would have to have an economic justification a little better than "Otherwise the government takes it."

The disbursement tax should be reserved exclusively for the Federal Government, and no similar form of taxation be allowed the states or localities. The tax rate should be set up from year to year, in accordance with budgetary requirements.

Revenue for the states should be derived from sales taxes and excises, road and bridge tolls, and from use taxes of all sorts on public facilities. Sales taxes, gasoline taxes, liquor taxes, motor vehicle registration fees, license fees of all kinds are in full operation now. They should be raised where it is necessary to bring in added revenue. Also, to avoid wasteful duplication of collection and administration, they should be reserved exclusively for the state governments.

Road and bridge tolls have proved highly successful revenue raisers. They should be extended to cover other public facilities now offered free, including education beyond elementary school. For the latter, we have the example of most civilized countries, which rightly believe that the community does not owe everyone a college, or even a high school education. With us, such free higher education is at present partly wasted on a fair percentage of its recipients, as any educational expert who goes by facts and not by theories will testify. A very broad and comprehensive system of state scholarships and state aid for truly deserving and promising students would ensure proper intellectual leadership, as it does in most of the world's enlightened nations, including even the Soviet Union. Suitable trade schools for the manually inclined would round out the picture, reduce the number of dropouts and give proper preparation for life to those who have neither equipment nor inclination for intellectual pursuits.

Localities should have reserved to them all real estate taxes and local license fees, and they should have the courage to raise and lower the tax rate and assessments in accordance with their requirements, instead of frantically casting about for new nuisance taxes as sources of revenue, or begging for state or federal aid. It's the same taxpayer who pays the bill, whether locally or through the devious process of having the federal or state government collect the tax revenue, then pass it back to the locality minus what Senator Goldwater has rightly called a brokerage fee.

In this fashion, we could achieve a logical, generally equitable, and altogether economic system of taxation and revenue-raising. The nation's tax bill would in effect be paid by every citizen, roughly in proportion to his means. We would get rid of the infinite duplication and triplication of taxes that appear today (federal income tax —state income tax—city payroll tax; federal gas tax—state gas tax—city gas tax; federal excise—state excise—city sales tax; etc.), with a consequent vast reduction of bureaucratic personnel and huge economy in government at all levels.

But most important of all, we would lift the dead hand of government from the individual, and make the latter truly free once more. None of the taxes we have described bears on the individual as such. All bear on things and activities which the individual is free to take or leave, in any given instance, without running foul of the government.

If We Must Retain The Income Tax

SHORT OF ABOLISHING THE INCOME TAX ALTOGETHER, AND replacing it with a more economical and less offensive form of taxation, is there a program of income tax reform that would apply to both the Federal Government and the states that have an income tax, bring in the necessary revenue, yet eliminate the more glaring injustices of the present laws, and, above all, ease the burden of the taxpayer for what concerns the time, labor and money he has to expend on his tax obligations, plus the invasion of his privacy by an inquisitive and inquisitorial bureaucracy?

Income is income. If we are going to retain the income tax principle, there is little that can be done to modify the definition of what constitutes taxable income, or its listing.

Something can definitely be done about capital gains. Here perhaps a 25 percent maximum, regardless of the time the asset is held, would be of signal help. It would eliminate the gamble feature that now attends the disposal of assets held for longer or shorter periods, and permit transactions to take place on the basis of their actual merits, and not on the basis of higher or lower tax rates.

Income spreading over a five- or even a ten-year period would eliminate the grosser injustices attending the taxation of incomes that show wide fluctuations from year to year.

Top rate for the federal tax should be set at 50 percent. There is no justification, moral or economic, for the government's taking more than half of what a person makes, unless we want it as a confiscatory and punitive measure, which is how it works today.

A 20-percent minimum rate is realistic under present-day conditions. What is not at all realistic, particularly for lowest income groups, is the personal exemption of $600 per capita. Who can live on $600 a year today? There is urgent need to restore the former exemption of $1,000 for a single individual, $2,500 for a married couple filing a joint return, and $500 for each dependent.

The 50-percent top rate for high incomes would affect the government's revenue very slightly. The higher personal exemption would affect it considerably. This means that the rates between 20 and 50 percent should not be cut, but raised if necessary.

The biggest desirable changes should come in the matter of allowable deductions, as well as in the manner of reporting them. It is here that 90 percent of the controversies between Internal Revenue and the taxpayer develop. It is here that the biggest work of checking and investigation has to go on. It is here that the biggest headache to the taxpayer appears, by reason of too much complication and confusion as to what is deductible, and the necessity of keeping unreasonably bulky records to prove his claim. It is here that the biggest loopholes result in the biggest loss of revenue to the government.

Either all taxpayers, big or little, should be allowed to take their choice between two tax rates, a higher one with itemized deductions and a lower one with no deductions; or a realistic standard deduction of at least 20 or 25 percent of declared taxable income should be optionally offered to all taxpayers, as is now done with incomes below $5,000 with the standard 10-percent deduction. The taxpayer would still have the choice of listing his deductions if he thinks he is entitled to more. But in such cases there should be an automatic, compulsory audit.

Let us not worry about the fact that this might work to the advantage of the wealthy. The wealthy, in the overwhelming majority of instances, are able to claim bigger deductions than the realistic standard here suggested, and make them stick, by reason of highly paid legal talent at their command, plus the contributions loophole. At any rate, the wealthy usually have expenditures of a deductible type roughly in proportion to their income. The millionaire miser, who would take advantage of the standard deduction to cut his contributions to worthy causes, was a rarity before the income tax era; he is even more of a rarity today.

But in addition, our sense of justice demands that drastic changes be made in the definition of what is deductible. For one thing, all income taxes, both federal and state, should be deductible, since they represent amounts that are not truly income. If my yearly income is $20,000 and $5,000 of this is withheld by my employer or paid out by me in quarterly installments on estimated tax, I am not getting $20,000; I am getting only $15,000. This principle, by the way, is fully recognized by union labor when it speaks of "take-home pay." The taxed-away portion of my nominal income should by all standards of justice and equity be deductible.

There is no good reason, on the other hand, why any other taxes, federal, state or local, should be deductible. They represent necessary adjuncts to expenditures which I am making of my own free choice. No one forces me to smoke, drink, drive a car, buy goods subject to sales tax, or own a private home. If I choose to do any of these things, I should shoulder the taxes incidental to them. The same principle should apply to interest payments I may make. These represent an item of my own free choice.

Medical expenses, on the other hand, do not represent an item of personal choice. They should be fully deductible, at any age level and for all dependents. So should life and health insurance premium payments, which are, in a sense, as much of an element of security to the community as they are to me, since they tend to guarantee that I and my dependents will not become public charges. All expenses connected with one's employment or the production of income, including travel to and from work, should be fully deductible. It is highly unfair to allow the business executive the use of an automobile for so-called business purposes (let alone the expensive entertainment of prospective customers in nightclubs or on yachts) and to deny the worker subway or bus fare, or the use of his car, to get to his source of income.

Lastly, I would suggest fully abolishing the deductibility of contributions. These represent an item of free individual choice and should be so treated. Every cent I deduct from my tax bill as a contribution to my church has to be made up for by other taxpayers who have other religious affiliations, or none at all. Every cent I pour into a charity, or a cause, or a foundation, has to be replaced by people who do not believe in that particular charity or cause. Churches, charitable and educational institutions, foundations not conducted for profit, are and should continue to remain tax-exempt for what concerns their property and income and the contributions made to them. This should suffice. The tax-deductible feature for contributions has probably been the biggest source of loopholes and loss of revenue to the government. Its basis is unfair, as it compels the general taxpayer to contribute in effect to activities he does not wish or intend to support. Such activities were in the past supported by their own believers and followers, and will doubtless continue to be so supported, even if the tax-deductible feature for contributions is abolished.

These suggested reforms of the existing tax structure are aimed at correcting gross injustices, while keeping the government's sources of revenue intact. They are aimed at relieving the taxpayer of the excessive burden of record-keeping and reports to which he is at present subjected, as well as at eliminating the ever-possible and occasionally present harassment of the individual by government bureaucrats who have to justify their existence by creating more paperwork for themselves and the community at large. They are aimed at putting the tax-gathering operation on a more rational and economic basis.

They should be very definitely coupled with the principle, enunciated by Governor Scranton of Pennsylvania in his inaugural address, that each individual type of taxation should be reserved for one branch of government, federal, state or local, and that there should be no overlapping forms of taxation. It is an economic waste and an unwarranted harassment of the taxpayer for both the federal and the state government to impose an income tax, or liquor and cigarette excises, or gasoline taxes, or for the state and the locality both to impose sales taxes. Economic realism and the convenience of the taxpayer demand that each type of tax be imposed and collected by a single government agency and that the governments have the courage to raise the tax rates for sources of revenue reserved to them in accordance with their needs, instead of casting about for new and imaginative sources to tap, which almost always turn out to be forms of taxation already in use by another branch of government.

The Secretary of Economy

TAXATION WITHOUT REPRESENTATION IS AN ABOMINATION. Taxation without proportionate representation is almost as bad. If we are to retain the institution of the steeply graduated income tax, there is need of some revision in connection with the way the taxpayers are represented.

In a stock corporation, stockholders do not vote as individuals, but in proportion to their holdings of stock. It is a recognized and obvious principle that the man who owns a million shares of General Motors should have more of a voice in the running of the corporation than the man who owns a hundred shares.

It is not at all desirable that this principle be carried over into our political life. Every citizen of the United States has an equal stake and an equal interest in the country, by the mere fact that he is a citizen.

Does this mean, however, that every citizen is justly entitled to an equal voice in the matter of revenue and expenditures, when one man may supply two-thirds of the revenue and a hundred others put together only one-third, and when each of the hundred requires individually a bigger outlay of the government's money than the one who supplies the bulk of the revenue? On a straight "democratic" basis, the hundred can always outvote the one. They can even vote for confiscation of the one person's total income, and its redistribution among themselves. This is ethically wrong, but constitutionally possible, unless we invoke the somewhat dubious "pursuit of happiness" principle. There is no provision, even in the Bill of Rights, on behalf of the sacredness of property as such.

Other nations have tried to solve in different ways the inconsistency between political democracy (one vote to each person, regardless of his property holdings or tax contributions) and the principle of the individual's financial stake in the proper running of the country. The single vote for every citizen, coupled with a plural vote for people with certain educational or property qualifications, has been tried, with debatable results. The poll tax, setting a price on the right to vote, is repugnant to the freedom-loving, as tending to exclude certain classes from the conduct of the nation's affairs. Equally repugnant, and for the same reason, is the right to vote subject to a property classification.

It would not be inequitable, however, to propose that among all our elected and appointed officials there should be one whose special function it would be to represent the interests of the taxpayers as such. In some Scandinavian countries there is the institution of the public defender, whose specific assignment it is to defend the individual from the encroachments of government and government officials.

The President normally appoints his own Cabinet, which is not subject to the choice of the voters, though there has to be Congressional approval for Cabinet appointees. This means that the party that controls both the Presidency and Congress usually has its own way. There could be added to the Cabinet, by constitutional amendment, an additional *elective* Cabinet post—a Secretary of Economy (not of *the* Economy!), who would be elected by the taxpayers on a plural-vote basis based on each taxpayer's individual contribution to the nation's exchequer; who would not be subject to removal by either the President or Congress; and who would represent the people who supply the revenue that makes the government function, in proportion to the amount of revenue each one supplies. For this official there would be a special election, every two or four years, at the time when the final yearly income tax return is due. In fact, the taxpayer-voter could register his choice on the return itself, though the various candidacies might be presented three to six months earlier. It would then be easy to count the votes from the tax returns. Corporations would register their choice in the same fashion as individuals, having previously polled their stockholders.

It would be the function of the Secretary of Economy to scrutinize budgets and proposed and current appropriations, voice his opinion publicly on the desirability and need of any proposed expenditure, and actively seek ways and means of reducing the government's expenditures without impairing the government's efficiency. The fact that the Secretary of Economy would be elected directly by the taxpayers, that he would be in no way responsible to the executive, legislative or judicial branches of the government, and that he would be elected for a very specific purpose, that of safeguarding the taxpayers' money, should render him absolutely fearless and independent. At the same time, he would have no executive or legislative power. The former would remain vested in the President and the rest of the Cabinet, the latter with Congress. Both the executive and the legislative branches could override the voice of the Secretary of Economy at will. But that voice would be heard throughout the land. Pork-barrel legislation, unwise and frivolous government spending, unnecessary appropriations would be widely publicized, instead of being buried in secrecy, as they often are at present. The taxpayers would know, and be properly aroused, as they should be. It is their money that is being spent.

All people and organizations that pay a federal income tax, big or small, without exception, would be entitled to one vote. The number of votes to which they are entitled would then rise, in accord with a definite formula, for those who pay larger amounts than, say, $100. One might suggest two votes for payers of taxes amounting to yearly sums between $100 and $1,000, with another added vote for every $1,000 beyond that.

The benefits that would accrue both to the nation's economy and to economy in government by the presence in the Cabinet of such an elected official could easily outweigh the advantages of a sweeping tax reduction unaccompanied by reductions in government spending.

The Unemployed Are Always With Us

IN THE DAYS WHEN I ATTENDED HIGH SCHOOL, MANY OF US boys found it necessary or expedient to seek gainful employment during the summer vacation period. The process was quite simple. You looked over the help-wanted ads in your favorite newspaper, picked out the likely looking ones, and presented yourself. You generally got your summer job the same day. It would pay you a more or less standard wage of $5 a week, whether you hired yourself out as an office boy in an importing house or law office, an errand boy in a Fifth Avenue shop or a bank, or whatever else was available.

Five dollars a week doesn't sound like very much today, but remember that its purchasing power in the days before World War One was easily five times what it is now, and that the idea was not so much for a boy of 14 to support himself with it, since we all lived with our families, but to gain experience and help out the family economy. My mother got my $5 a week, and gave me carfare and lunch money.

Even after graduating from high school, I recall that jobs were not at all hard to find. Again, they would not pay much, by modern standards, even after making allowance for the greater purchasing power of the dollar. My first elementary school teaching post, at the age of 17, was compensated at the rate of $60 a month and lunch. Later, a three-month job as floorwalker in Macy's paid me $22 a week.

There was work for everyone, if you cared to accept it at those rates. The only unemployed were those who couldn't or didn't want to work.

The Great Depression, of course, changed all this, and after it came the Roosevelt Era and World War Two. Since then, we have had a perennial minor problem of unemployment.

Five million unemployed, in an economy that employs over seventy million, is not too bad. Part of it is accounted for by loafers, relief chiselers, job shifters. A couple of million are technologically unemployed, by reason of automation or the death of certain industries, coupled with unwillingness to move to another locality where there are jobs. The worst aspect of our current and perennial unemployment seems to be that it strikes hardest at young people just out of school. They find it harder to land jobs than older, more experienced workers.

Is there a reason for this? I think we'll find it if we care to look into conditions of employment in the horse-and-buggy days and now.

To begin with, the current youngster out of school, with no experience, scorns any job that pays less than $65 a week. Certainly, with the cost of living and taxes what they are today, you cannot expect him to work for the old $5 a week, or even for the $25 that more or less equals its purchasing power. But when you make allowance for everything, he still wants twice as much as we did, for the same type of work. Yes, the general standard of living has gone up. Today everybody has to have a car, a TV set, and a lot of other things we lacked. Still, one wonders. As between a low rate of compensation and being unemployed, we preferred the low rate of compensation.

But there is another factor, one which involves not the employee but the employer. In hiring an extra office or errand boy back in the early 1900's, the employer incurred no risk or liability beyond the payment of that $5 a week. He did not have to consult a union or pay union wages, take out sickness or unemployment insurance, make federal and state tax and Social Security deductions, or otherwise get himself involved. He might hope that the boy he hired would learn the business, stay with the firm, and eventually become a senior and valuable employee. But if he didn't, it didn't matter much. The arrangement was one that could be terminated any time, at the will of either party. It involved nothing beyond the payment of that weekly wage. And what firm or business organization could not find some use for an extra boy at that price and under those conditions, even if only to get Volume 75 of the *Southeastern Reporter* out of the firm's law library and carry it to the desk of the junior law partner, or to be sent out to buy the afternoon paper and a container of coffee?

Today, things are vastly different. An employer must think twice and three times before he takes on any sort of employee, even an office boy. It involves all sorts of paperwork, reports, responsibilities. All this the employer is willing to put up with if the employee is one he really needs and can't do without. But to go through all that rigmarole for a youngster who may or may not stay on for the duration of the summer vacation, or who has to be trained and then quits after he gets his training and goes somewhere else? Is it worth the trouble? Is it any wonder that the junior law partner prefers to do it himself and get his own volume of the *Reporter* out of the library, that the credit manager prefers to step out and buy his own paper from the stand, that the corner grocer prefers to make his own delivery of the loaf of bread and quart of milk ordered by telephone?

Labor unions have done the country a signal service in bringing up the general standard of living and giving dignity to the workingman. They have done it a signal disservice in eliminating jobs that ceased to be economic after the unions appeared on the scene, and in driving business concerns to the extremes of automation long before they would normally have done so.

Not being an economist, I cannot estimate how many elevator operators' jobs were eliminated by the push-button lift. But being an observant observer, I can truthfully state that there was a great rash of push-button lift installations after the great New York elevator operators' strike. Landlords, tenants and business firms were firmly resolved that they wouldn't be caught napping again. Yet the elevator operator, plus a doorman, used to be a great source of protection to dwellers in apartment buildings; a push-button can't give warning of a holdup man, or protect one from a rapist.

Once upon a time, before the days of Mr. Quill, elevated and subway trains had a guard between every two cars, to operate the doors manually; incidentally, they were also numerous enough to keep order on the train, and located in such a way that no act of vandalism or crime would go unnoticed. Today, one man with a push-button opens and closes the doors of a ten-car train; if he stands in the middle of the train, he has no way of knowing what goes on in the last car, and being all alone, save for the motorman, he has no way of opposing an entire gang of hoodlums.

Once upon a time, city trolleys and buses had a motorman or driver, whose sole duty it was to run the vehicle and watch the traffic, and a conductor who collected fares, made change, gave directions. Today the same man does both, and it is a wonder even more city bus drivers don't get nervous breakdowns, let alone ulcers.

It is easy to say that automation would have come along anyway, and people be thrown out of work by it. But what economist will inform us precisely to what extent automation has been speeded and made imperative by labor union demands that either were excessive or at least impressed employers as being impossible to meet? Automation may pay for itself in the long run, but it's a long run, and it is my belief that many, many employers, particularly in the smaller businesses, would have gone on indefinitely under the old system if they hadn't been forced to automate by union demands they could not meet and still operate at a profit.

So now we have labor union members who are employed (when they are) and draw comparatively large wages. And we have an undetermined number of people who could be employed at lower rates of compensation if this were not made impossible. Since these people have to be kept alive somehow, the community, which is theoretically saving the low wages they could be enjoying (along with their own feeling of satisfaction and self-respect), puts them on relief and is out the same amount of money, but with demoralizing side effects.

Recently I spent ten weeks in Portugal, a backward country by our standards, and definitely a poor one. You saw beggars, but they were the blind and the halt and the lame, people who really could not work. On the other hand, you saw a great many people, most of them elderly and uneducated, who held small jobs as gardeners (Portugal is one vast public flower garden, and its government proposes to keep it that way), or as custodians of state monuments, showplaces and buildings. Apparently everyone who is able to do some work, be it ever so light, is given a job with a wage, be it ever so small. These people smile and are seemingly contented. They are not charity recipients. They have their self-respect. In fact, they are government employees, in some kind of uniform, and are proud of their humble role in the nation's life.

By way of contrast, during a hard winter spent in Pittsburgh, where over 20 percent of the available labor force was unemployed and drawing some form of relief or other, there was no one to clear the crosswalks, let alone the streets, of snow and ice. Would it have been un-American to demand that able-bodied, unemployed steelworkers on relief do a little snow shoveling, perhaps even at added compensation? Apparently it was.

Yet Portugal's Salazar, who used to be professor of economics at the University of Coimbra before he assumed the reins of power, was scathingly described by an American liberal of my acquaintance as "the man who ought to be holding the chair of eighteenth-century economics." If eighteenth-century economics means keeping the people employed and giving them a sense of human dignity instead of throwing them a relief or Social Security boondoggle and breaking down their morale, I'm for it.

Government and the unions seem to have entered into a conspiracy to hold down the number of available jobs by eliminating all the ones that don't pay a wage that is princely by any other nation's standards (the $1.50-an-hour minimum wage law is an illustration); by making it very difficult for an employer to take on a youngster fresh out of school, or for a housewife to hire domestic help; by discouraging people between 65 and 72 from taking on the light occupations for which they would still be fitted if they are in good health (see the provisions of the Social Security Law).

All this is supposed to be good for us by giving us the highest standard of living in the world (which we had achieved, by the way, long before the days of New Deals, Fair Deals, New Frontiers and Social Security).

Actually, what it does is to give some of us big wages and salaries that are perhaps out of line with the services we perform; but for these, we have to make up by high taxes designed to take care of that part of the population which we willfully force out of employment. In addition, it deprives us of public services to which we should feel entitled, but about which no one seems to worry.

All this has been pointed out and described in detail by Galbraith in his *The Affluent Society*. He does a much better job of description than I could hope to do. But his remedy seems to be: "Accept the situation, and learn to live with it. There is nothing you can do about it. Resign yourselves to having half of the population permanently unemployed, and supported by the other half, who work far harder than they ought to. But they like to work, while the drones don't."

My suggested remedy is different. Turn back the clock. Make it possible once more for an inexperienced youngster out of school to be taken on, even if he doesn't quite get $100 a week for his services. Make it possible for the man over 65 to draw the Social Security to which he is entitled, having paid taxes on it in his earlier years, and still not be penalized for holding down a light job, such as elevator operator or night watchman. Take the able-bodied man off relief, and give him instead a regular job doing something that needs to be done, even if it is only keeping the streets clean of rubbish and clearing the crosswalks of snow. The cost will be approximately the same; but even if it is slightly higher, isn't human self-respect worth something?

Make employment possible by getting rid of such bureaucratic trappings as income tax and Social Security withholdings, unemployment insurance, union dues, government reports, for all occasional and petty jobs (one might suggest in this connection that the full paraphernalia of bureaucratic reports go into operation only after a person has held a job for six months, and has achieved a wage level such as to warrant the suspicion that what he makes might be subject to taxation).

After all this is done, we shall still have our aged and infirm and unwed mothers and orphaned children and perennially unemployable, as well as our job shifters, who need not be counted as unemployed. But that is the residue that any civilization, however advanced, must take care of. Certainly three million such people, out of a population of 200 million, need not constitute a major worry.

V

Education

Justice For The Teen-Ager

AS A MAN WHO ONCE TAUGHT ELEMENTARY AND SECondary school for close to twenty years, I know that there is one quality above all others that the growing boy wants and respects in the grown-up world. That quality is not "love." It is not "sympathy." It is not even "understanding," save in a special sense. What he really wants and respects is justice.

Not justice in the wishy-washy sense in which it was once outlined by a young and enthusiastic assistant district attorney to a panel of the New York Grand Jury on which I sat. We listened in growing amazement and skepticism while he described the wonder-working plan whereby youths of 14 to 16, guilty of serious crimes, were given a little lecture, then remanded in the custody of their parents, and even had their names erased from the police blotter, so that they would not suffer "psychological traumas" comparable to the physical outrages they had visited on others.

The kind of justice the teen-ager wants is that which is prescribed by a code that he must follow, under penalties that need not be cruel or unduly severe, but must have the certainty of retribution. To such a code he will subscribe, as proved by both the gangs and the Army. When the youngster gets into either, he does not violate their codes, because he knows they are rigidly enforced. He wants a system of rewards and punishments, with the as-

Originally published under the title "Teen-Agers Don't Require 'Understanding' As Much As Discipline and Responsibility" in *Saturday Evening Post,* this article was reprinted in dozens of newspapers and periodicals, including *Reader's Digest* (under the title "What Young People Need") and all the international editions of *Reader's Digest.*

surance of both. This is because he considers himself to be not a child, but an adult.

There is nothing wrong with his point of view. The age of reason, of discrimination between right and wrong, is normally set at the age of seven. Beyond that age, and often before it, the normally endowed individual knows what he is doing. What is more, he wants to be responsible for it.

Successful teachers (and parents) are those who recognize this fact, set down the law, and stick to it. It doesn't have to be—in fact, it shouldn't be—a harsh law. Merely a just law, universally and rigidly enforced. Treat the youngsters, from age seven up, as normal human beings. Tell them what is expected of them. Tell them what will happen if they don't live up to it. And see that it unfailingly happens.

Give the kids a sense of law and justice, along with a sense of normal human responsibility. Don't encourage them to think of themselves as irresponsible "children," beyond the reach of law and discipline, and therefore authorized to do anything that enters their minds without restraint or inhibition. Let them know that they are responsible for their own actions, and that "underprivilege" is no more of an excuse than "overprivilege" is a license to do wrong.

In the days when I went to school we were taught that the roster of America's great men is filled with people who came up from abject poverty, from the log cabin and the big city slum. In a free society like ours, no one is bound by his environment who really wants to rise above it. Throw a little bit of that good old American guts back into the schoolroom and the home, and back it up with some real faith in the American principle of individual responsibility.

Back in the days of the American Revolution we threw out the old-world belief in superior and inferior classes, particularly the former. In recent times we have been tending to reestablish it by an implied belief in an inferior, irresponsible class destined to remain forever inferior and irresponsible because of background and environment. It's time to reverse that trend.

If we let each growing child, each teen-ager, know that he is on terms of absolute equality with all others, in the sense that he is free to rise or fall, be rewarded or punished, in accordance with his own efforts and achievements, the fundamentally wholesome youth of America will respond, as it has never failed to respond in the past.

It would be idle to deny that there are many subsidiary causes of juvenile delinquency—economic insecurity, broken homes, alcoholic parents, the influx of new racial strains, TV programs, movies and comics that glorify crime. But they, or their equivalents, were there in the past, too. At the most, they may account for a minor percentage of the evil. So long as we go on blaming everything on social inequities, economic underprivilege, "tensions" and "frustrations," we shall get deeper and deeper into the mire.

The cooperation of everybody is needed—parents, teachers, ministers of God, police authorities, judges; in fact, all adults, and all teen-agers, too. What we most need to do to cure the spiritual disease of youthful crime is to secure the cooperation of the patients themselves by setting up real, undeviating standards of rights accompanied by duties, discipline accompanied by individual responsibility, law accompanied by justice—the things a teen-ager can respect.

Russia's Secret Weapon

THE RUSSIANS HAVE AT THEIR DISPOSAL A SECRET weapon, not recognized as such by our keenest observers, which tends to give the Russians a disproportionate advantage over us. Despite the fact that they started the in-

Acknowledgment is hereby made to *Modern Age*, where this article originally appeared, for permission to reprint the piece here.

dustrial race fifty years after we did, that their economy does not and cannot function as well as ours, that they lack a firm foundation for moral principles, having renounced God as a source of ethics, they nevertheless enjoy a tremendous superiority over us which we need not at all allow them to retain.

Their big advantage lies in the field of education. Their secret weapon consists of the fact that they are using, by and large, the educational methodology and point of view that we discarded fifty years ago, in favor of the will-o'-the-wisp of progressivism, permissivism and "life adjustment," to which we cheerfully sacrificed discipline, respect for authority, content and subject-matter, and the formation of individuals rather than cogs in a machine.

The last item may sound strange, in view of the fact that we are supposed to be the individualists, they the subordinators of the individual to the all-powerful state. Yet in the field of education their present system, like our system of half a century ago, tends to form a complete, well-rounded individual, equipped with those items of information that really matter, and therefore intellectually free even if politically and economically enslaved, while our present system places far too much stress on the individual's adjustment and conformity to his sociological environment, and too little on the development of his power, as an individual, to rise above that environment, think for himself, and select his own reactions to life's problems.

Fifty years ago, the schools of this country, like the Soviet Union's today, were firmly based on discipline and respect for constituted authority. Self-discipline can arise in the immature mind only as the result of discipline imposed from without, and gradually relaxed as the individual develops, until the day comes when it is no longer necessary. To abolish discipline and respect for authority in the immature mind is tantamount to condemning that mind to remain forever immature. The American child fails to grow up as he advances in years. The result is the utter irresponsibility and aimlessness, the vandalisms and hoodlumisms, the juvenile delinquency we so often deplore, but of which we persist in ignoring the true basic causes—lack of respect for parental, church, school, even government authority. It will avail little to say that such authorities are occasionally unworthy of respect. They were so then, as they are now. But by and large, the parent, the teacher, the priest or minister or rabbi, the policeman or truant officer, are superior to the youngster, if only by reason of age and experience. This superiority, of course, is neither inherent nor everlasting. It will and should gradually vanish as time rolls on—but only gradually, and as time rolls on. For parents, teachers, juvenile court judges, to make themselves, or rather pretend to be, the equals or even the inferiors of the growing children is a ridiculous procedure, which is studiously avoided in the Soviet Union, but unfortunately widespread here. Children are still children. They should be lovingly, but firmly treated as such while they remain children, at the same time that they are lovingly, but firmly taught the principles of individual responsibility from which so many of their elders shrink.

The old-style school, like the Soviet school of today, was a place for learning, and the learning tended to be factual. It did not attempt to be all things at once—church, home, social center, pleasure palace, sports arena. Extracurricular activities, proms and dances, athletics, discussion clubs, were limited in number and scope. What the school did, it did thoroughly and well. It did not turn out graduates who could not yet read, write, spell or do simple arithmetical operations. It was taken for granted that social adjustment (whatever that term may mean), physical culture, sex life, would largely take care of themselves on the outside and at the proper time. The student's main job was, as the name would seem to imply, to study, not to discover how to go out on a date, cheer for the team, or complain about living conditions that are today incommensurably superior to those of fifty years ago.

The Soviets are turning out of their schools young people who are in all respects but one similar to those we turned out in the first decade of this century—people who are well informed, self-reliant, willing to work—the raw material out of which a successful society is built. The one important respect where they differ is the matter of political indoctrination and conformity. In that one and very important respect, we are still their superiors, though even that is tending to disappear by reason of government meddling in our educational system. Our younger generations are poorly prepared for what concerns factual subjects, indoctrinated with an exaggerated sense of their own importance and what the world owes them rather than what they owe the world, an impatience to arrive too far too fast, coupled with a lack of the intellectual means to get there, a built-in tendency to conform unthinkingly and uncritically to fads and mass standards.

The children of today are the men and women of tomorrow. Judging from present indications, the Soviet Union of thirty years hence will have a population of political robots who will, however, be well equipped intellectually, be capable of initiative, hard work, self-discipline and self-sacrifice. We will have a population of highly nervous, not to say neurasthenic people, uninclined to work, effort or sacrifice, poorly equipped in factual knowledge, tending to follow mass standards of conduct and worship material things, whose only advantage will reside in the fact that they still have left a modicum of political choice, a sense of discrimination for what concerns their leadership, and some shreds of continued belief in a God-given moral code.

What We Don't Know About The Russians *Will* Hurt Us

"IF YOU HAD ONLY TAKEN THE TROUBLE TO READ OUR scientific journals, you would have known all about our

In somewhat abridged form, and under the title "Science Students Should Know One Foreign Language," this article appeared in *Saturday Evening Post.*

plans to launch the first sputnik at least a year before it was launched."

The speaker was Professor A. I. Mikhailov, Director of the Institute of Scientific and Technical Information of the U.S.S.R. Academy of Sciences. His listeners were a group of American scientists attending a news conference in Washington, where Mikhailov was a visitor.

His words came as no surprise to them. In October, 1957, after the first Russian satellite hit outer space, there was a wild scramble to translate and read piles of Russian scientific journals that had been gathering dust on the shelves of our university libraries and government offices. They at once revealed the awful truth—that the Russians had made no secret whatsoever of their intentions and experiments.

Since sputnik, there has been a spasmodic, belated effort to arouse more interest in language study, particularly in the study of Russian, so that we won't get caught napping again. This effort, as at present conducted, is largely wasted, at least for the purpose for which it is intended.

Acquisition of a foreign language does not automatically make you a qualified translator in the scientific and technological fields. The man who knows two or more languages well enough to speak them fluently, understand them readily, read them currently and write them well is still not automatically equipped to translate a scientific document. He must also know, and know thoroughly, the field with which the document deals. The literary translator, who can put Pasternak into English and Hemingway into Russian, is almost as helpless as you, the reader of this, in the face of a piece of written material dealing with mathematics, electronics, nuclear physics, or even automotive construction. He is as helpless as was the present writer, a fluent speaker of several languages, when he was confronted with a technical banking document that was to be translated into English from Italian, the two languages he knows best and in which he has written dozens of books and articles.

Each scientific and technical field has a terminology of its own—generally clear, precise, unmistakable to the specialist in the field. But this terminology is so much Choctaw to the nonspecialist that it might as well be an unknown tongue. If you doubt this, open at random a book on a technical subject you have never studied, and see how fast you get lost. You have a far better chance of success at reading an ordinary work of fiction in French after a year of high school French than at reading a book in English on thoracic surgery, the structure of the atom, or what makes a rocket go—unless, that is, you have actually studied seriously, and for a considerable period of time, these topics.

This, by the way, is partly true even of nonscientific topics—the law, business, finance, art, music. Every specialized field has its own extensive vocabulary, its own language clichés, its own set of customs, and these, like driving rules, differ from field to field, as well as from language to language. You may know how to drive a Chevrolet like an expert in New York; but try, without previous preparation, or a knowledge of French traffic rules and signals, to drive a Peugeot in Paris, and see how many tickets you accumulate in the space of an hour.

All this adds up to one conclusion. It is not enough for us to get more people to study and read foreign languages. Those people must also be the people who know the scientific fields in which we want them to use their linguistic talents. In other words, we must have a scientist and a linguist combined in the same person.

Of course this is revolutionary. We have always had plenty of people who go in heavily for the sciences. Despite Russia and sputnik, we still have the best engineers and technicians in the world. We have also always had people (not quite so many, perhaps) who go in for one or more foreign languages. What we have never, or very seldom, had is a combination of the two.

Our science specialists may, at the most, take a year or two of some foreign language, then promptly proceed to forget what they have learned, because there is so much for them to concentrate on in their own scientific field. Our language majors, on the other hand, practically never have an interest in science. They regularly go in for grammar, literature, philology, and the teaching of more grammar, literature and philology. Our technical translators, people who know a scientific field thoroughly and at the same time know a foreign language well enough to handle in it material in their own field, are a handful. You'll find most of them concentrated in a few technical translation bureaus, where they eke out a living by doing translating jobs for such business firms as may have an occasional need for their talents.

The Russians have thousands of them, if not hundreds of thousands. Their future scientists are required to take eight to ten years of one foreign language in addition to specializing in a scientific branch. This means they learn that foreign language well enough to speak, understand, read and write it. But above all, they learn it well enough to translate into it and from it the special jargon of their own scientific specialty. Therefore the Russians not only receive some 13,000 technical periodicals from all foreign lands (including about 1,400 from ours); they also read them carefully, and if they find anything of particular interest, translate it at once and bring it to the attention of the proper authorities. This we don't do. Result: sputnik, announced by the Russians a year in advance of its appearance, comes to us as a complete surprise and shock; and "us" includes both American scientists and American government.

About fifteen years ago, a well-known technical lexicographer, Lewis L. Sell, published a book, to which no one at the time paid the slightest attention, advocating the creation of an institute for the training of technical lexicographers, translators and interpreters. We needed that institute then, and needed it badly, but we didn't know it, because we thought we were so far ahead of the rest of the world in science and technology that what other nations thought or did was no concern of ours. Now we need it even more badly, and now we know that we have formidable rivals. It is still not too late to do something about it.

But in addition, we need a different slant on our very belated and somewhat frantic attempts to expand language learning. It is not enough to get a few more students into our high school and college language classes, and teach them how to read Françoise Sagan in the French original, or even *Doctor Zhivago* in Russian. What we have to do, if we want to make sure that foreign scientific achievements won't come to us again as a big surprise and an unpleasant shock, is to make thorough specialization in at least one language an essential part of our scientific and technological training. There is no reason why an American electronics or chemical engineer can't be fluent in Russian, when his Soviet counterpart is fluent enough in English to be able to pick our brains at will.

VI

Ethics, Public and Personal

Moral Amnesia and Collective Guilt

ONE OF THE MOST DISTRESSING SIGNS OF OUR TIMES IS the loss of individual moral sense, the consciousness of individual responsibility for our own actions. One of the most felicitous phrases ever coined to describe this phenomenon is Ruth Nanda Anshen's "moral amnesia"—forgetfulness of one's obligations, and of the moral code that has guided us in the past. It is as though a great many among us had drunk of the waters of Lethe, and gone into a state of utter oblivion, a rosy world in which no one has to face the burden of one's own deeds.

Crimes, often of a revolting nature, and behavior that would at one time have shocked society and aroused indignation even to the point of violent action, now go unnoticed and often unpunished. We accept as part of normal living the unsocial conduct of individuals and groups, shrug our shoulders at incidents that range all the way from widespread relief cheating and preposterous legal suits that run up insurance costs, to teen-age vandalism, rumbles that often have fatal consequences, and gangsterism that blossoms into crime syndicates and Murder Incorporated.

Criminal tendencies, once sternly repressed, are excused on the ground that the criminal is young, immature, insecure, a product of social conditions. Courts, law-enforcement agencies, organs of public information enter into a conspiracy of silence to cover up the most dastardly deeds. A young married woman is assaulted by three youthful hoodlums, forcibly dragged to a roof, raped, then stomped to death to keep her from revealing the identity of her assailants. The criminals are apprehended. Two of them turn out to be what the courts call "juvenile offenders"; their identity remains undisclosed, and they are presumably remanded to children's court. At this point the newspapers and newscasts lose interest in the case. What may have happened after that is anyone's guess.

This moral amnesia is by no means restricted to our own country. Neither is it limited by class differences. Prominent political office-holders are among the worst offenders in condoning lawlessness for the sake of votes. There is a disgraceful giving in to the pressure of minority groups that happen to hold the balance of voting power in certain areas. Tax inequities are justified on the flimsiest grounds, and new and extortionate taxes are imposed by states and localities with the extenuation that they will not weigh as heavily upon the individual as they seem to at first glance, because they are deductible from the individual's federal income tax.

In the international field, where might has always made right, past practices are continued and expanded, but with the sanction of new, sanctimonious international bodies. After being told that aggression would be a thing of the past once we had such organizations as the United Nations, we are treated to the spectacle of such aggression carried on in Goa and West Irian, not by the old, wicked colonial powers, but by the new, lily-pure Asian states of India and Indonesia, without even a word of censure. Having been regaled with the unjust Nürnberg trials, where all principles of international and natural law were violated by the fact that the victorious powers set themselves up as both judges and juries when their only justifiable role was that of prosecuting attorneys, we have witnessed a further, astounding exemplification of the new legal-moral code in the Eichmann case, where the guilty party, instead of being extradited by due legal process, was kidnapped from the soil of the nation where he resided, and tried, condemned and executed by the victims of his crimes instead of by neutral parties. Such sublimations of the doctrine of lynch law seemingly shocked very few people, least of all those who are most vocal in deploring the old-style lynchings of the West and South, where the victims of the lynchings were often just as guilty of the crimes of which they were accused as were Göring, Ribbentrop, Laval and Eichmann.

But in return for our lost moral sense of individual responsibility, a new and even more frightening doctrine is offered us, the doctrine of collective and inherited guilt.

In accordance with this doctrine, people who are no longer personally responsible for their individual actions become personally responsible for the collective doings of the national, racial or social group to which they belong. Here we see the fine hand of world Communism, with its "class enemies," persecutions and mass deportations of recalcitrant groups, both national and social.

According to this doctrine, the Germans (all Germans without exception) are guilty of the crimes committed by Hitler and his Nazis. Plans for their collective punishment were offered at the end of the war, ranging from the proposal to de-industrialize Germany and condemn that country forever after to lead a backward agricultural existence to the suggestion that all living Germans be taken on a forcible tour of Dachau, Buchenwald and Auschwitz to view the horrors of those places and acquire a sense of personal guilt which a good many of them, having had nothing to do with perpetrating those atrocities, and having been in no position to oppose them, did not have.

Actually, it is difficult to see what "good" Germans could have done about Nazi crimes while the Nazis were in power. The few who tried to make their voices heard found themselves persecuted and shot, exactly like the Jews they were trying to save from extermination. All men are not heroes, as proved in our own country by the difficulties experienced by law-enforcement agencies in trying to secure courageous witnesses, willing to risk their own and their families' lives, in connection with the prosecution of known gangsters. Faced with overwhelming and unscrupulous force, most "good" Germans thought discretion was the better part of valor, precisely like most American shopkeepers victimized by the rackets.

Even now, it is sometimes deplored that the new German generations, those who were either children exposed to the Allied bombings of Berlin and Hamburg, or actually unborn at the time of the war, fail to feel personally responsible for Hitler's doings.

It would be equally reasonable to expect all Americans to feel personally responsible for the atom bombs of Hiroshima and Nagasaki. Those of us who were living at the time did not even know of the existence of the atom bomb until it went off. I, and, I feel certain, millions of other adult Americans with me, refuse to accept responsibility for military top-level decisions made without our knowledge or participation. And who could expect our teen-agers to feel an overwhelming sense of guilt for what was done in 1945?

The pernicious doctrine of collective responsibility and inherited guilt is now employed by the enemies of our traditional moral code on two separate fronts, the international and the internal. Internationally, it takes the form of African and Asian pressures for what might be styled "reparations" for a colonialist past. Self-righteous spokesmen for the "fledgling nations," aided and abetted by the weak-minded in our own midst, are at great pains to tell the nations of the West that reparations are due the newcomers because they were once colonialized and occasionally mistreated. It is forgotten by these nations that they themselves had been, were, and in many cases still are guilty of identical practices. Foreign conquest and oppression are so commonplace in the course of history that they may be described as the rule rather than the exception in international relations. The North African Moors colonialized Spain and Sicily at one time, and should not consider it a moral offense if the French turned the tables on them at a later period in Tunisia and Morocco. Attila, Genghis Khan and Tamerlane are there to show what the yellow races can do in the way of armed aggression.

Nazi atrocities of the genocidal variety in the course of the last war have been duplicated in the not too remote past by the mass slaughter of Armenians conducted by our present friends the Turks. Even the French need to be reminded, by a showing of Goya's paintings if nothing else, that the "liberating" armies of Napoleon were no gentler with the guerrilla fighters of Spain than were the Germans with the *maquis* of the *résistance*. Yet no one advanced the thesis that the French were subhuman after Napoleon fell.

On the internal front, we are asked to harbor a sense of national, collective guilt for the fact that our Negroes were once enslaved. It is perhaps too easily forgotten that hundreds of thousands of whites gave up their lives to free them from an enslavement which was at the time generally practiced everywhere, often with Europeans and even Americans as the victims. (Our war with Tripoli was caused by the delightful North African custom of attacking merchant ships in the Mediterranean and selling the crews into slavery on the North African markets.)

It is far too often forgotten that colonialism and slavery, reprehensible as they were, had their good as well as their bad effects. Would India and Indonesia, Nigeria and Ghana be better or worse off today if the colonial powers had not brought to them the blessings as well as the curses of Western civilization? Is it altogether an accident that the Arab population of Algeria, roughly one million when the French took over in the 1830's, numbers over ten million today; or did French medical science and engineering and agricultural skill make it possible for that population to expand? Would India and Indonesia be unified nations today had the British and the Dutch never been there? Or would they still be fractioned off into the innumerable despotic principalities they were before the Europeans came? Had it not been for the Yankee slave traders and slave clippers, most of our American Negroes would not be alive today to clamor for the civil rights to which they are entitled. Their ancestors were largely prisoners of the most warlike tribe on the West African coast, the Ashanti, who ate their captives when they couldn't sell them for trinkets.

The fact of the matter is that the past is replete with injustices and atrocities for which we of the present cannot be held accountable. But we can, and should, be held accountable for our own personal, individual behavior. One act of unwarranted injustice or violence on my part directed against a fellow human being, whatever his color, race or affiliation, makes me infinitely guiltier than all similar acts committed by others in the past or in the present.

The doctrine of national and collective guilt should be recognized for what it is: a Communistic propaganda weapon cunningly devised to weaken our morale, throw us into confusion, and disrupt the unity that should prevail among all who believe in individual freedom coupled with individual responsibility.

The Cult of Trash

I HAVE A FRENCH FRIEND WHO CLAIMS THAT THE FALL of France in 1940, with the breaching of the Maginot Line, the collapse of the French Army, previously rated as the best in the world, and the occupation of the entire country by the Germans, was a direct consequence of the indoctrination of the younger French generations with the demoralizing philosophies of such authors as Gide, Proust and Sartre.

It is probable that something more was involved. But the degeneration of literary and artistic standards is undoubtedly a contributory cause to the downfall of a nation. In all events, such degeneration is a symptom of general moral decay. We have seen it happen too often in the past history of the world.

This is not a plea for stuffy Victorianism in art and literature. Neither is it advocacy of restrictions on artistic and literary forms, such as those inaugurated by Hitler and Stalin in their respective countries. Artists and writers must be free to create and express themselves, if art and literature are to endure as free entities, and not become mere appendages to political systems.

Least of all is it advocacy of censorship and Comstockism, repugnant to all free spirits. But it is advocacy of the return of reason and good taste to the artistic and literary scene. And the rebirth of reason and good taste must start with the consumer, which is the general public.

After all, if there were no buyers there would be no sellers. If there were no takers, there would be no prostitutes. In a sense, the problem of literary and artistic taste is one of simple economics. But simple economics is interfered with by publicity, ballyhoo, and criticism with an ax to grind. The public very often is given very little choice. It has to take what is offered. What is offered is all too frequently determined not by merit, but by someone's preconceived or interested notions as to what the public wants.

This, of course, is the basis of the infinitely bad taste of most TV and radio commercials. Someone sells the sponsor the idea that the public is "sold" by a loud, blary, screechy jingle whose words no one can understand because they are covered up by the noise, or by suggestive images of carefree young men and women who are "having fun." The legend is repeated and perpetuated. Soon there is an entire chain of trashy commercials, in strident contrast with the frequently excellent programs. The sales theory becomes a tradition, then an article of faith. "That's what the public wants!" After that, there is no turning back.

Something similar has been going on for decades in numerous fields: art, sculpture, architecture, music, and, above all, the stage and literature. Trash has become enshrined. The trash runs all the way from the merely valueless to the actively harmful. At the best, it corrupts standards of good taste. At the worst, it corrupts a nation's moral fiber.

Consider, for example, the cult of trash as exemplified by what goes on in the twin representational (or formerly representational) fields of painting and sculpture. All one has to do is glance at the art page in the Sunday *New York Times,* or wander up and down the circular ramp of the Guggenheim Museum. Here are forms of so-called art that either resemble the scrawlings and mud-pies of idle children or produce a definitely revolting effect. (One of the world's truly great contemporary artists reports that on his first viewing of some "modern" works he went out and vomited; later, he says, he got used to it.)

The critics will tell you seriously that this is art—impressionistic, or nonobjective, or nonrepresentational, or futuristic, or cubistic, but art nevertheless. Prizes have been won by paintings produced by the artist dipping his feet in paint, then stepping all over his canvas. Other paintings have won prizes by the simple expedient of being hung upside down; actually, by the time the show was on, no one, not even the artist, could tell any more which side was up and which was down. There are samples of a few straight lines drawn across a canvas which is otherwise blank; circles, or dots and dashes, or spikes, or cubes. Sometimes the artist tells us what his creation is supposed to betoken, sometimes he leaves it to our fervid imagination; after all, our guess is as good as his, particularly if he has produced his work by dipping his dog's tail in paint and then letting it wag over the canvas.

In "sculpture," two wires are twisted together and the result is labeled "Naked Girl Emerging from the Bath." Or a sphere is placed on top of a cube, and we are left to give the object our own name.

Yes, real beauty is occasionally achieved in the nonrepresentational field. In the Student Hall of Schenectady's Union College is a room hung with nonrepresentational works produced by the students themselves which to me have far greater beauty by reason of their ingenious use of color than most of the prize-winning pieces in New York's museums. They don't sell. They are fantastic enough, but not sufficiently crazy or in bad taste.

Does the general public like these forms of art? There is no telling. They are favored by the vanguard longhairs. But the real point is that they are taken seriously by the art critics, and in consequence bought, sometimes for thousands of dollars, by people who have too much money.

In architecture, we get some creations, like those of Frank Lloyd Wright, that are fantastic; others, like the

UN Building, that seem to me downright ugly. But architecture has a practical as well as an aesthetic function, and functionality may be the justification for the ugliness, or even for the fantasy.

Unlike music, which is by nature symbolic, art and sculpture are basically representational. At least they started out that way. They are supposed to tend toward realism and reality, to portray what is in nature. It took the human race a long, long time to achieve realism in those fields, as indicated by the imperfect representations of some ancient and most medieval art and sculpture, as well as those of backward groups. It would seem that having once fully achieved the ability to portray nature, the artists and sculptors would be satisfied to leave it that way, and exercise their ingenuity in the direction of seeking new subject matter. Not at all. They seek forms of expression that mark a reversion to a backward stage, or to downright infantilism. And the critics and buyers go right along with them.

Nor will it avail to say that art must achieve and reflect motion. If motion is wanted, there is nothing better than a motion picture. Perhaps a certain artist was right when he moved out of painting into photography, on the ground that painting had gone through its full cycle, and could now mark nothing but a regression.

I once listened to an interesting discussion concerning objective *vs.* subjective art criticism. The artist who led the discussion held that both were possible, in the nonrepresentational as well as the representational field.

It was my contention that only subjective criticism was fully possible in the nonrepresentational division of art and sculpture. If a straight line across a blank canvas or two pieces of wire stuck together are meaningful and beautiful to the art critic, who am I to argue with him as to his own aesthetic taste? But by the same token I claim the right to assert that they are neither beautiful nor meaningful to me, because I, like all other human beings, am also endowed with an aesthetic taste.

But in the representational field, I held and hold, there are objective standards, dictated by the similarity or lack thereof that the art work bears to what it purports to portray. The work of art is good to the extent that it faithfully reflects nature. The more a painting or sculpture looks like a real human body, or a real sunset, the better it is, in the objective artistic sense. The nonrepresentational artist, therefore, makes a mistake when he gives a naturalistic label to his work, and expects us to accept it as the portrayal of the object described in his title.

Could it be that some of our moderns go off the deep end of distortion because they despair of being able to duplicate the feats of Michelangelo in sculpture, or Raphael in painting (or, for that matter, Gounod in music and Shakespeare in literature)? Could it be that their so-called artistic output is merely the externalization of one vast, overwhelming inferiority complex?

In music, after achieving heights of symphony à la Beethoven and opera à la Verdi, we are now in the downswing. It is not merely our popular music, our jazz and twist stuff, that carries us back to the tom-tom of the African jungle (in fact, some of our popular music, of the rock-and-roll and hootenanny type, has definite charm, on a lower plane). It is rather what passes by the name of modern opera, modern symphony, modern chamber music, marked sometimes by bi-tonality, sometimes by the absolute lack of melody and harmony. It is quite true that music, being altogether symbolic and not at all representational (unless one wishes to record a sound track of a factory in full swing, or the cacophony of a jungle), offers the greatest possibilities of artistic leeway and individual aesthetic choice. (Here I am reminded of the popular Italian story of a Turkish dignitary who was taken to the Rome Opera to listen to his first operatic performance; at the close, he was asked what part of the opera he had liked best; it turned out to be "the very beginning," where the musicians were tuning up their instruments.)

Still, even in music there is the possibility of achieving symmetry of sounds, rhythm, sequences that catch and please the ear. All this goes by the board in most modern offerings.

Again, there is an economic aspect to the question of musical taste. I have often wondered why some compositions of (to me at least) very scanty merit make the headlines while others of exceptional worth fall by the wayside, being either unpublished and unplayed or overlooked by the critics and by those who should bring them to the public notice. Why, for example, all the hullabaloo about Menotti's *Saint of Bleecker Street* or *The Medium,* productions that are torture to the ear, and the complete silence that enveloped Maurice Baron's *François Villon,* an opera of exquisite, almost unearthly beauty, produced once on the radio and then forgotten? Does the public really have a chance to show its preferences when the publicity mills get going, or fail to go?

True, the public, which in music has to have a broader base than in art, has a chance to show its preferences, and does so in no uncertain fashion with works that are fully and traditionally available on the market. Compare the number of performances and the attendance at *Aïda* or *Trovatore* with the corresponding phenomena at *The King's Henchmen,* or Beethoven night *vs.* Hindemith night at the Lewisohn Stadium.

It is strange that the realism that is so studiously avoided in modern art should be sought after in modern literature and on the modern stage. Here, in the name of realism, we are treated to views of all the degrees of depth of human degradation, along with unnecessary graphic accounts of all physiological functions, interspersed with a choice four-letter vocabulary, repeated ad nauseam and wallowed in as buffalo would wallow in mud.

Hemingway's *Old Man and the Sea,* for instance, was labeled a great work of literature. I have never been able to see it that way, but that is neither here nor there. Why, however, does Hemingway have to inform us on repeated occasions, in the course of his short book, that the old man urinated over the edge of the boat? These episodes add absolutely nothing to his work of description of a mental state or what have you. It is not as though the old man was suffering from prostate trouble, and that was essential to the story. Could the reader not be trusted to assume that these things normally happened, as they normally do? Just how is the cause of realism advanced by these trite, overworked, overlabored descriptions of things that are infinitely and wearyingly universal?

But "realism" in literature goes much further. Nobel and other prizes are awarded to writers whose major merit is that all, or most, of their characters are depraved, with their depravity unrelieved by good traits. In the rare instances where they are not depraved, they are just plain trashy. I remember seeing *Tobacco Road* for the first time and voicing my skepticism that even in the backwoods one could stumble across a complete set of such worthless characters. Faulkner's *Sanctuary* made a similar impression upon me, as did *A Streetcar Named Desire*.

The all-time high for literature seems to have been achieved by a French writer, Genet (I haven't read him yet, and may not get around to reading him, having better uses for my time), who is described as an illegitimate child who never knew his parents, who was sent to the reformatory for stealing at the age of ten and thereafter served time in the jails of every country he visited over a thirty-year period. After ten convictions for theft, he was sentenced to life imprisonment, but pardoned through the intervention of France's leading artists and writers. He is now acclaimed as one of the most prominent figures in European literature. One critic describes him as "the most brilliant, the most gifted, and the most depraved" of the new French writers. Sartre says of him "we are confronted with a regression toward infantilism, toward the childish narcissism of the onanist," that he "starts by enveloping himself in his images, as the polecat envelops itself in its odor." His work "smells of bowels and sperm and milk"; "with fiendish application it leads human creatures to downfall and death"; "here is the complete and unshackled expression of an utterly evil and decadent mind, set down with a kind of grotesque pride and in entire honesty." The final judgment concerning his masterpiece, now thrown on the American market, is expressed by a great literary critic: "The greatest novel he or probably anyone else has produced in the last twenty years." All this marks our progression in literary taste.

Of another native work which has recently had trouble in American courts, one court decision states in part: "Experiences not ordinarily pictured as related to sexual motivations are analyzed in flights of surrealistic fantasy in terms of sexual experiences. . . . The book, in narrating the author's stream of consciousness, necessarily expresses the writer's thoughts in their most primitive aspect, often violent and repulsive, and constantly in four-letter words."

The remedy for this literary frame of mind is not censorship, but copious doses of that very realism in whose name these literary crimes are committed. We are ready to admit that people such as are described in these works exist. We will even admit their right to be described. But the implication of those who describe them goes much further. It is to the effect that *all* people are like that, and that is not true.

Some people are depraved by nature; others fall from grace; but it is my contention that the overwhelming majority of people are decent, in all walks of life, and in all social classes. Realism demands that they, too, be depicted. Between Pollyanna, Rebecca of Sunnybrook Farm, and *Little Women* on the one hand, and the prize-winning masterpieces we have sketched above on the other, there should be a middle ground. Even Horatio Alger had his villains. Even Tennessee Williams should have his decent people.

But the mills of publicity are what they are. There is a shock value to a pornographic tale, and it doesn't have to be good to sell. A tale that is not pornographic, on the other hand, has to have real literary merit to appeal to the public. It is so easy to gain success with prostitute stories, like *Irma la Douce* and *Never on Sunday,* which turn a social sore into an object of laughter, or with "funny" films, plays and stories about death, like *The Trouble with Harry* or *Arsenic and Old Lace*. But death is no fit subject for humor. Prostitutes, homosexuals, narcotics addicts are to be viewed with pity, not made the object of ridicule. At any rate, these manifestations, while they are real enough, ought not to be made the sole goal of literature, to the exclusion of more exalted sentiments.

The latter are deliberately excluded from the modern literary field, which is dominated by the sophisticates.

There was once an account of boyhood reminiscences involving the sentimental reaction (but it was authentic enough) of the main character to the American flag, which he viewed as a symbol of love and protection extended by a great nation to those who sought shelter under its banner's folds. "How corny can you get?" was the comment of a literary agent, who knew, from long experience with publishers, whereof he spoke.

Realism in literature has yet another foe, what Ivor Brown describes as Zero-worship. This refers to the meaningless, uninteresting, inarticulate character who muddles through a story, but doesn't get anywhere much. Modern books are often replete with such characters and their listless doings, meaningless utterances, and what passes for thoughts. Salinger's *Catcher in the Rye* is to me a perfect example.

Then there is the cult of deliberate obscurity, fostered by many modern poets, who reject all rhyme and reason, "turning words into barbed wire, behind which they dug themselves in to resist all efforts at interpretation of their deeply buried thoughts and purposes," and extended to prose writers of the Faulkner persuasion, who occasionally forget themselves and write well and clearly for a page or two, then realize their mistake and quickly retreat behind their smoke screen.

Reputations in Mr. Brown's literary "anti-world" are often achieved by leaving stories unfinished, so that the question: "What happened to these people?" is left unanswered. An outstanding example is supplied by Gadda's *Quer Pasticciaccio Brutto della Via Merulana* (*That Ugly Mess on Merulana Street,* now out in English translation), which starts out as a fairly plausible whodunit, then ends suddenly while the noose is tightening around the man suspected of committing the crime, in the very midst of an interrogation of a witness by the detectives assigned to the case. It is not too hard to figure out the rest, but why should the author try to impress his readers in this fashion with his marvelous psychological profundity? Yet this work was widely hailed as a masterpiece of prose when it first appeared.

Other widely advertised and prize-winning works of prose, without going to these lengths, leave you altogether cold as to the ultimate disposition of the characters. Who cares what happens to *The Moviegoer?* Or even to the motley crew of *Ship of Fools?* Of the latter, an unofficial poll taken among well-to-do women college graduates revealed that practically all of them described the work as "inferior to my expectations" ("which were not very high anyway," one reader volunteered to add).

I repeat that the antidote for the cult of trash in literature and poetry, which is by no means restricted to our own country, does not lie in censorship, prohibitions or expurgatory indices. It lies in selectivity and the exercise of literary taste on the part of the reading and viewing public; sales resistance to the blandishments of the publishers' propaganda mills; definite comments on the part of book readers and movie- and play-goers as to what they want and do not want.

If every reader of a book in which he is disappointed, every viewer of a movie or play that shocks his aesthetic or moral sensibilities, were to write an irate letter to the publisher or producer of the offending piece of trash, there is no doubt that standards would rise.

There is such a thing as too much public tolerance of the inane, the banal, the distasteful and the harmful. Passivity on the part of the consumer is not a virtue. Writers, producers, publishers, will be quick to change their tune once they find out what it is that the consuming public really wants, and learn to distinguish it from what the ax-grinders in their midst tell them it wants.

What Every Man Has To Give—His Level Best

YEARS AGO, IN THE DAYS BEFORE AUTOMATION FELL upon us, I lived in an apartment house which still had manually operated elevators. One of the uniformed operators was a handsome, middle-aged Negro whose first name was Louis. He was friendly, helpful, courteous; but so were the other men.

What particularly drew my attention to him after a time was the fact that when he ran the elevator he invariably brought it to a straight stop on an absolute flush with the floor level. The stop at the floors was not automatic, and a hit-or-miss procedure could result in the spread of an inch or two between elevator and floor level, with a consequent courteous warning to "please watch your step," "step up," "step down." Louis, I observed, never had to issue these warnings. His stops were always perfect.

"How do you manage it, Louis?" I asked him one day with a smile. "Manage what, Professor?" he smiled back at me. "Make such a perfect landing every time." He smiled a little thoughtfully. "You see, Professor, back in the days when I went to school there wasn't too much chance to go on to higher education. I took a job running an elevator when I was seventeen. It gave me a pretty good living, and I kept on doing it. Since I wasn't doing anything else, I thought I'd learn to do it right. I studied that elevator until I knew all its tricks. I've done that with every elevator I've ever run. It's not hard if you really try."

He paused for an instant, then went on. "I believe that

whatever people do, they should do well. It may not amount to much in the case of any one man, but if everybody did his job right this would be a better world to live in."

Eventually, I convinced Louis to do some studying in his spare time, and he finally took a civil service exam and became an employee of the Post Office. I haven't seen him in many, many years.

But he stuck in my memory, and still does. I do not know where I have learned a more enduring lesson, or acquired a better piece of philosophy than I did from my friend Louis. "Whatever your job is, high or low, do it right! Do it well! If everybody did his job right, this would be a better world to live in."

We cannot all be scholars or intellectuals, or even white collar workers. We can't all occupy big, important posts. All men are equal in the sight of God, but He has not seen fit to endow them all with equal equipment. To some He has given more brains, to others more brawn, a better physique, better health, a more cheerful disposition, a more fetching personality.

But this He knows. All He requires is that we use to the best of our ability the equipment He has given us. One, five, ten, a thousand talents, what does it matter? What matters is that we put to work, honestly and faithfully, the talents entrusted to us.

The man who mastered the art of running an elevator to the point where he could make a perfect stop every time is in God's eyes the equal of the man who runs well the affairs of an entire nation. He is entitled to the same dignity and respect as a good President.

Envy or Emulation?

IT IS EASY AND NATURAL FOR US TO ENVY THOSE WHO are seemingly more fortunate than we. It is equally easy to attribute their success to sheer luck.

Once I knew a man who had devoted considerable time and effort to learning the more intricate portions of contract bridge. He bid shrewdly and played well. He often played with a circle of friends to whom bridge was merely a pastime. He won more often than he lost. As often as the scores were added up, and he came out on top, there would be a chorus of howls from the others: "The luck of the guy!"

Another acquaintance of mine had put in long hours at his chosen profession. He was successful. His success made him the object of envy of the circle he moved with. "How lucky he is!" was the general comment as he came out with a new successful idea.

Of course the element of luck cannot be discounted. It very frequently plays a preponderant role in the affairs of men, and of nations as well.

But everything is not luck. Success is just as often the result of careful, painstaking preparation, agonizing labor, unstinting time put into an endeavor, of whatever nature.

When this happens, it is unfair to speak of luck. It is particularly unfair when it comes from people who are, as the saying goes, "happy-go-lucky," and who rely not on their own initiative and efforts, but on "some lucky break turning up at the right moment."

At any rate, envy is not a virtue. In some religious denominations, it is one of the seven capital sins.

Its antidote is properly directed admiration and, where the circumstances warrant it, the spirit of emulation. It is no sin, surely, to admire success, study it, strive to imitate it and achieve it.

When we are tempted to envy, or, what is close to envying, attribute all success to the element of sheer luck, let us first study the situation. Envy may have some justification when its object is a sweepstakes or roulette table winner, though even here it might be argued that a bonanza or windfall, being purely material and unconnected with its recipient's efforts or merits, is unworthy of envy.

But where effort, application, hard work enter the picture, the proper attitude is one of admiration. Above all, the right kind of success should arouse in others the desire to emulate, to prepare and strive as hard and as long and as doggedly.

Do not seek objects of envy. Seek objects of admiration and emulation. And before you say you never have any luck, examine your conscience carefully. Have you done everything you should have done? Have you exerted maximum effort? Has everything gone wrong in spite of the very best you could possibly do? Then, and only then, are you justified in speaking of bad luck.

Words That Change One's Life

IT IS NOT DIFFICULT FOR A PERSON WHO IS AT ALL LITERate to run up a fairly impressive list of books and writings that he considers masterpieces of beauty of expression or plot, pieces of literature that to him stand head and shoulders above the merely good or entertaining, and may be deemed worthy of immortality.

My own choice in the matter runs mainly to the poets, for poetry supplies an element of rhythm that confers upon writing some of the aesthetic qualities of music. Since I can read some (by no means all!) of my favorite poets in the original, my aesthetic enjoyment is capable of going beyond that of the man who is restricted to a single language. I can admire Homer's choice of sounds in Greek and Virgil's majestic sweep in Latin, the severe rhythm of Dante and the unearthly imagery of D'Annunzio in Italian, the measured cadence of Pushkin and Lermontov in Russian, the euphonic harmony of Camões in Portuguese, the staccato lilt of Schiller in German, the haughty grandeur of the *Cantar de Myo Cid* in Spanish, as well as the infinite expressiveness of Shakespeare and the jingling breathlessness of Poe in English. And when it comes to works that I must read in translation, what can compare for depth of feeling and sheer exotic loveliness with the twin glories of medieval Persia, Omar Khayyam and Hafiz?

But these, and many others that could be added, are works designed to please the ear and arouse the admiration of the mind. The works that give inspiration to the spirit are far, far fewer. Fewest of all are those of which one can truthfully say: "These writings have struck me so hard that they have forced their way into my philosophy, and changed my outlook and my life."

Other things besides books and writings have this God-given faculty, of course. It may be the spoken word of a sermon or a conversation or an admonition. It may be a piece of music, or a work of art or architecture, or the contemplation of a landscape. It may be a natural phenomenon like the dawn or the twilight, a sun-drenched mountaintop or a moon-filled night, the tranquil or stormy sea, the fleecy clouds scampering across the blue sky and the fresh wind that chases them like a sheep dog.

But in most of these some of the interpretation and inspiration comes from within. Only in the written and spoken word does the stimulus come entirely from outside of us, impinging itself upon our consciousness as a consciously delivered message, complete in all its parts, so that we may not only receive it, but calmly evaluate it and be altogether free to accept or reject it. By virtue of its symbolic, all-pervasive power, the word is indeed God. And the written word has over the spoken word the immeasurable advantage of being fixed and permanent, so that one may refer to it again and again, go back to it as one would go back to a wellspring in an oasis, to draw from it new yet perennial refreshment.

At the risk of being considered corny by the scoffers, I will set down those writings, no more than one could count on the fingers of a single hand, that have brought about a change in my outlook and my life, given me a fresh perspective, influenced my thoughts and actions. I honestly believe that all my readers have at some time or other shared this experience, even though they may have forgotten it, and be only subconsciously influenced by it.

Perhaps what I have to say will bring it back into the focus of their consciousness. If this happens, I shall consider myself well repaid for my effort.

From my high school days, I remember being impressed by a passage in one of Cicero's Orations, appropriately enough the one delivered on behalf of Archias the poet. Cicero the lawyer, quickly glossing over the facts in the case, bases his defense of his client, who had been accused of fraudulently obtaining his Roman citizenship, on the supra-legal principle that poets and poetry are sacred and above the law. He cites example after historical example to prove that they have always, and among all races, been held holy. As he approaches his peroration, he makes a personal confession to the jury. Archias has promised his defense counsel that if there is a verdict of acquittal he, Archias, will immortalize Cicero in verse. This is Cicero's coveted legal fee, and he rises to impassioned heights of eloquence to gain it.

What has man to look forward to, save the boon of immortality in the memory of posterity? Cicero wants desperately to be remembered after his body has turned to ashes. All men worthy of the name, says Cicero, are spurred on by the hope of praise and glory; in fact, they seek no other reward.

"Surely, if man's spirit had no feeling about the future, and limited its interests and longings to what is encompassed by life's span, it would neither wear itself out in difficult tasks nor distress itself with cares and worries nor so often consign itself to a life-and-death struggle. But in every decent man there is a quality which spurs him on night and day with the goad of glory, and warns him that the memory of his name is to be equated not with the duration of his life, but with all that will follow him. We, who have suffered and striven for the public weal to the point where we die without ever having drawn a peaceful breath, cannot be so small in spirit as to imagine that everything will die with us. Others have left monuments to commemorate their bodies; ought we not to prefer bequeathing the effigy of our achievements in polished verse? Even as I labored, I was inspired by the thought that I was sowing my labors like a seed into the field of man's everlasting memory. Whether my consciousness will abandon me after death or, as many wise men have thought, continue to remain a part of my spirit, I assure you that as of the present moment I cherish both the idea and the hope that the memory of me may endure."

Cicero was a pagan. He did not have the assurance of individual survival after death that Christianity gives us. His hope (and it was an unselfish, even selfless one) was merely that he might live on in the annals of mankind and the minds of men. He sought a noble recompense for his labors, and he received it.

Further Classical studies in college brought to light new treasures of literature and philosophy. But one gem of wisdom remained particularly fixed in my memory and colored my subsequent thoughts and actions. It is a series of admonitions voiced by Horace to some of his acquaintances who were inclined to avarice.

"You hoard up wealth, my friend, but to what avail? What will you do with it when death comes to you, as it must come to all men? And even while you live, of what real use is it to you? Though you own all the grain from all the threshing-floors of Libya, your belly can hold no more than mine. Though a hundred purple Syrian robes hang in your closets, you can wear only one at a time.

"You say you know values. Do you really know what the value of a *nummus* is? Have you any idea of its real worth? Bread can be bought with it, to feed the hungry, wine to assuage the thirsty, clothing to cover the nakedness of the poor."

I have always thought that one cannot read those simple sermons of a pagan poet, not touched by Christianity, without realizing the futility of selfishness, the stupidity of basing one's life and efforts upon material things alone, the essential need of man to consider the needs and wants of his less fortunate fellowmen.

Graduate school brought medieval French into my purview, and with it a work that I consider, rightly or wrongly, as the greatest masterpiece in all French literature, the *Chanson de Roland*.

It is easy to view this work, as do the majority of literary critics, as a mere account of blood and thunder, the story of a partly historical, partly legendary military episode in the life of Charlemagne.

Spiritual, psychological elements are regularly overlooked in this grim description of Charlemagne's retreat from Spain, the treason of his brother-in-law Ganelon, the destruction of his nephew Roland's rear guard in the pass of Roncevaux.

Roland is viewed as a hothead who needlessly sacrifices the 20,000 men under his command because he is too proud to call for help. The story is thereby turned into a medieval version of the Alamo or Custer's Last Stand.

Seldom do the literary critics venture into an interpretation of motives and outlook, or pause in their examination of minute military details to realize that the semi-anonymous author of the *Chanson de Roland* was bequeathing to posterity not merely an entrancing, pulse-quickening tale, but a set of standards, values and rules of conduct.

For the *Chanson de Roland* is first and foremost an account of the loyalty and devotion that one owes his God, his sovereign, his country, his family, his superiors and followers. Though there is appeasement in the story, the spirit of Roland is not one of appeasement, or compromise with evil. "Pursue the war until the enemy is brought to his knees, no matter what the cost!" urges Roland in the face of the Moslems' false peace offer. It takes the hothead, the man of impetuous but rash courage, to see through the deceitful, cunning blandishments of the enemy. The *Chanson de Roland* is recommended reading for all those who think you can peacefully coexist with a treacherous foe who is determined to bury you, and who has proved time and again that he is not to be trusted.

Roland is proud and boastful when the battle starts, but his comrade Oliver, who has a better sense of strategy, warns him that the odds are too great. When Roland persists in not calling for reinforcements, Oliver warns him again: "Who fights this battle fights no other!" But Oliver and all the doomed men of the rear guard fight on to the finish, in the face of their own certainty that there is no surviving the Moslem onslaught. There is no surrender, no armistice.

"For one's liege lord one must be ready to endure heat and cold, to lose of his hair and blood and flesh!" says Roland. The spirit is that of the Battle of the Bulge, not that of Korea.

Roland's death on the battlefield is preceded by his touching plea to God for forgiveness of all the sins he has committed during his lifetime. It is followed by the death of Aude, his betrothed, when she learns from Charlemagne that Roland is dead. The mighty monarch offers her the hand of his own son as compensation for her loss. "May it not please God, His Saints or His Angels, that after Roland's death I remain alive!" is her reply. This episode is recommended to all those who under the guidance of Gide and Proust and Sartre and Tennessee Williams and Faulkner have transformed the sacred rite of love between the sexes into an orgy of self-gratification.

The *Chanson de Roland* may be taken as a mere account of battle if one be so minded. It can also be taken as a lesson in loyalty and steadfastness and adherence to one's code of honor and ideals, no matter what the odds.

The Simple Prayer of St. Francis of Assisi next comes to mind. For sheer literary beauty and imagery it is surpassed by the Canticle of the Creatures, where God is thanked for the simple things of this life, the sun and moon and stars, the earth and water and fire and wind, even death. But the Canticle offers no standard of conduct, save for the general admonition to thank God for His blessings. The Simple Prayer is far more precise, and needs no commentary:

"Lord, make me an instrument of Thy peace; where there is hatred, let me sow love; where there is injury, pardon; where there is doubt, faith; where there is despair, hope; where there is darkness, light; where there is sadness, joy.

"Divine Master, grant that I may seek not so much to

be consoled, as to console; to be understood, as to understand; to be loved, as to love; for it is in giving that we receive, it is in pardoning that we are pardoned, and it is in dying that we are born to eternal life."

I have deliberately reserved for my final sample the book that all Christians hold sacred, and that is indeed all things to all men, for in it one can find whatever one seeks.

Its moral lessons are so numerous that one could not list them here. Out of them all, one might choose the Parable of the Talents as a guide to conduct, were it not for the fact that there the standard, however lofty, is nevertheless a human one.

But Jesus, having the nature of God as well as of man, also sets for us superhuman, divine standards. One of these is the standard of judgment and forgiveness.

In the episode of the adulteress He speaks the words: "Let him among you who is without sin cast the first stone."

Ultimate judgment rests with God, not with man, because only God can plumb the depths of a human heart and soul. We have the right to formulate our own judgment, based on the elements in our possession. We have even the right to act upon that judgment, if it be honest and sincere, for life is a practical thing.

What we may not do is to pass ultimate condemnation in the moral field, or, better yet, arrogate the interpretation of motives. At all events, the story reminds us that whatever be the wrongdoings and weaknesses of others, we, with wrongdoings and weaknesses of our own on our consciences, must be merciful in thought and action.

Jesus Himself sets the example when He says: "Go, and sin no more." And later, as He dies that we may live, He adds: "Father, forgive them, for they know not what they do."

"This I Believe"

I BELIEVE THAT NEXT TO DIVINE GRACE, GOD'S GREATEST gift to man is time; not time to fritter away, but time to use to the best advantage of one's fellowman, and for the full development and fruition of those talents with which one has been blessed.

The proper utilization of one's time-span calls for the development of that sense of personal initiative and personal responsibility without which man sinks to the level of a cog in a machine. All men are not endowed with the same talents and abilities; but I believe that there is incumbent upon each individual an obligation to realize to the utmost the good and useful qualities with which he is endowed. In the realization of this obligation lies the fundamental truth of the proposition that all men are created equal. This basic equality of men in the obligation to put forth their best effort flows from their Creator; it knows no boundaries of race, nationality, religion, economic status, educational level, or political belief.

I believe that every human being has been given his own spark of immortality, and it is up to him to see that this spark does not die. I believe that every human being possesses the God-given dignity of individuality, and it is up to him and all other men to respect it. In the final analysis, man is not responsible for his actions to his fellowman, who may be as imperfect as he is; he is responsible to God, Who will ask an accounting for whatever gifts have been placed in trust with each of us.

Time is ill-spent to accumulate wealth, power or learn-

This essay is the script of a broadcast given in Edward Murrow's series by the same title on WCBS Radio. It has not appeared in print before.

ing if these things are looked upon as having value for their own sake. It is well spent if they are gained for the ultimate purpose of service to others. When the hour comes, as it must to everyone, to part from life's blessings, the question will not be how many of these earthly blessings have been gathered and are now being left behind, but to what use they have been put while the choice was ours to make.

The field of the accumulation of learning is the one with which I am most familiar. Here I have often been struck by the sterility of much of that accumulation, the indifference to the practical utilization of the wisdom and lore that have been so painstakingly piled up. The scholar who gathers wisdom not to make it available to his fellowmen who hunger for it, but to hoard it so that it may die with him is like the miser who buries gold in a secret place where no one may ever find and use it.

When I face my Maker, I know that the list of my shortcomings will be painfully long; but this, if nothing else, is what I hope may be seen on the credit side of the ledger:

He made full and proper use of the time and talents allotted to him;

He showed respect for the rights and dignity of his fellowman;

He acted in accordance with his sense of individual responsibility, never shirking his duty as he saw it, and never relying on others to perform the tasks assigned to him;

What little he had to give out, he did not attempt to hoard, but dispensed it with freedom and generosity;

He directed his efforts in such a way that when he left the earth it was, even though to an infinitesimal degree, a better place than when he entered it.

For this I strive, because this I believe.

MENTOR

Recent MENTOR Books You Will Want to Read